YESHUA BEN YOSEF

What the prophecies reveal about Mashiach

BRUNO SUMMA
2020

YESHUA BEN YOSEF
What the prophecies reveal about Mashiach

For permissions: brunosumma@yahoo.dk
IG: @torat_yeshua

Other books from the same author:

-The knowledge of good and evil
Summa, B. 2018 All rights reserved

-The Torah to the Galatians
Summa, B. 2019 All rights reserved

-Torat Yehoshua: According to the Hebrew book of Matthew
Summa, B. 2019 All rights reserved

-Pirkei Yaakov: A Jewish mystical view on the book of James
Summa, B. 2019 All rights reserved

-The TORAH Ethics: Commandments for every men
Summa, B. 2019 All rights reserved

First publish: January 2020

CONTENTS

INTRODUCTION

The wisdom found in the word of God is one of the few things that really amazes me. The mysteries within the Torah, within the prophets and within its stories are an infinite source of wisdom and knowledge. When the Tanakh is studied in the right way, using the right tools, it is possible to understand the whole plan of redemption elaborated by God even before the creation of the world, and certainly, it includes Mashiach and each one of us.

There is an ancient Christian custom of holding on to some Old Testament prophecies in order to prove Yeshua's redemptive work. Of course, it would not be otherwise, as the Gospels themselves rely on them to prove Yeshua's messianism. What we see today is the direct connection made by christian scholars between prophecies and the deeds performed by Yeshua; connections totally understandable to any human mind due to their obvious fulfillment in his life as state by the gospels.

Although the interpretations and a direct comparison between the prophecies and the earthly life of Yeshua is very valid, the spiritual side, that is, the reason why a specific prophecy was made, "why did it have to be that way?", are often left aside due to the lack of insight into what is hidden behind the words of the prophets.

The purpose of this book is to bring a Jewish vision about Mashiach and a study of the secrets hidden behind the words of the prophets with the intention of linking them with the life and work of Yeshua in order to be possible to understand what he meant when he presented himself as Mashiach and the reasons for having fulfilled certain prophecies the way he did.

This book will bring an approach using the biblical Gematria and several rabbinic commentaries on the secrets behind the prophecies mentioned in the gospels and fulfilled by Yeshua. In them, we shall see a much greater depth than simple deeds and facts; we shall see personal, ministerial and, above all, characteristics of the true mission and facet of Yehoshua Ben Yosef Hanotzri.

When it becomes possible to understand future events, such as the coming of Mashiach for example, when the Torah reveals to us who he really is, his mission, his deeds, it is a charming and a transforming thing; for that reason I was inspired to write this book, a result of many years of study and dedication to the commandments of God. I want to make clear that this is not an easy to understand book, it is not a book that should be read, but rather studied. A brief knowledge of the Hebrew language and some familiarity with the rabbinic language will be very useful to the reader when reading its content. The exposure of the studies will be as clear and direct as possible so that the true message behind the prophecies may be quickly absorbed.

MASHIACH

Many people who follow jesus, consider him the Messiah and know that to be the Messiah is to bring salvation to humanity, but that does not define exactly what Mashiach is. As many know, the Hebrew word Mashiach means "anointed", because he was chosen and anointed by God to lead. The word "Mashiach" appears 39 times throughout the Tanakh and the belief in its coming is part of the 13 foundations of the Jewish faith as described by Maimonides.

Mashiach will have God-given authority to govern all the nations of the world, impose His Laws, teach the Creator's true will, put an end to iniquity and bring the true meaning of human creation. Therefore, a faith in a messiah who abolished the Torah is to believe in a mythical being created by human minds, which is no different from the paganism in the ancient times.

Our sages teach that two Mashiach will come, the first is the suffering Mashiach and the second is the exalted Mashiach. However, there will not be two Mashiach, but only one Mashiach with two different facets in two different times.

> *Rabbi Yehoshua Ben Levi said: one will come as the son*
> *of man and the second on the clouds of heaven.*
>
> Ein Yaakov, Sanhedrin 11:49

The term MASHIACH is a term that denotes someone who is anointed and chosen by God, anointed and chosen to be a prophet, a priest and especially, the king. This understanding comes from some prophecies spread across the Tanakh, prophecies that deal with the end of times and the redemption that God will bring over all men:

> *In the days to come, The Mount of the LORD's House Shall stand*
> *firm above the mountains And tower above the hills; And all*
> *the nations Shall gaze on it with joy. And the many peoples shall*
> *go and say: "Come, Let us go up to the Mount of the LORD, To*
> *the House of the God of Jacob; That He may instruct us in His*
> *ways, And that we may walk in His paths." For instruction shall*
> *come forth from Zion, The word of the LORD from Jerusalem.*
> *Thus He will judge among the nations And arbitrate for the*
> *many peoples, And they shall beat their swords into plowshares*
> *And their spears into pruning hooks: Nation shall not take up*
> *Sword against nation; They shall never again know war.*
>
> Isaiah 2:2-4

But a shoot shall grow out of the stump of Jesse, A twig shall sprout from his stock. The spirit of the LORD shall alight upon him: A spirit of wisdom and insight, A spirit of counsel and valor, A spirit of devotion and reverence for the LORD. He shall sense the truth by his reverence for the LORD: He shall not judge by what his eyes behold, Nor decide by what his ears perceive. Thus he shall judge the poor with equity And decide with justice for the lowly of the land. He shall strike down a land with the rod of his mouth And slay the wicked with the breath of his lips. Justice shall be the girdle of his loins, And faithfulness the girdle of his waist. The wolf shall dwell with the lamb, The leopard lie down with the kid; The calf, the beast of prey, and the fatling together, With a little boy to herd them.

Isaiah 11:1-6

In these prophecies we can see various missions that will be accomplished by Mashiach, he will restore Jerusalem, gather his people to worship Adonai, wars will end, nations will be judged, there will be a leader from the tribe of Judah who will make that judgment, the Kingdom of Israel and the Kingdom of Judah will be once again reunited and His people will be brought back from exile.

The word of the LORD came to me: And you, O mortal, take a stick and write on it, "Of Judah and the Israelites associated with him"; and take another stick and write on it, "Of Joseph, the stick of Ephraim and all the House of Israel associated with him." Bring them close to each other, so that they become one stick, joined together in your hand. And when any of your people ask you, "Won't you tell us what these actions of yours mean?" Answer them, "Thus said the Lord GOD: I am going to take the stick of Joseph, which is in the hand of Ephraim, and of the tribes of Israel associated with him, and I will place the stick of Judah upon it and make them into one stick; they shall be joined in My hand." You shall hold up before their eyes the sticks which you have inscribed, and you shall declare to them: Thus said the Lord GOD: I am going to take the Israelite people from among the nations they have gone to, and gather them from every quarter, and bring them to their own land. I will make them a single nation in the land, on the hills of Israel, and one king shall be king of them all. Never again shall they be two nations, and never again shall they be divided into two kingdoms. Nor shall they ever again defile themselves by their fetishes and their abhorrent things, and by their other transgressions. I will save them in all their settlements where they sinned, and I will cleanse them. Then they shall be My people, and I will be their God. My servant David shall be king over them; there shall be one shepherd for all of them. They shall follow My rules and faithfully obey My laws. Thus they shall remain in the land which I gave to My servant Jacob and in which your fathers dwelt; they and their children and their children's children shall dwell there forever, with My servant David as their prince for all time. I will make a covenant of friendship with them, it shall be an everlasting covenant with them; I will establish them and multiply them, and I will place My Sanctuary among them forever. My Presence shall rest over them; I will be their God and they shall be My people. And when My Sanctuary abides among them forever, the nations shall know that I the LORD do sanctify Israel.

Ezekiel 37:15-28

In Ezekiel's prophecy there are some other factors about Mashiach. Ephraim (son of Yosef) will be reunited with Judah by a leader originally from Judah, a prince, a king, the one who will restore the Holy Temple. With that, it is possible to see some things about Mashiach, the priestly aspect of Mashiach (Levi), the redeeming aspect of Mashiach (Yosef) and the royal aspect of Mashiach (Judah).

I looked up, and I saw four horns. I asked the angel who talked with me, "What are those?" "Those," he replied, "are the horns that tossed Judah, Israel, and Jerusalem." Then the LORD showed me four smiths. "What are they coming to do?" I asked. He replied: "Those are the horns that tossed Judah, so that no man could raise his head; and these men have come to throw them into a panic, to hew down the horns of the nations that raise a horn against the land of Judah, to toss it." I looked up, and I saw a man holding a measuring line. "Where are you going?" I asked. "To measure Jerusalem," he replied, "to see how long and wide it is to be." But the angel who talked with me came forward, and another angel came forward to meet him. The former said to him, "Run to that young man and tell him: "Jerusalem shall be peopled as a city without walls, so many shall be the men and cattle it contains. And I Myself, declares the LORD, will be a wall of fire all around it, and I will be a glory inside it. "Away, away! Flee from the land of the north, says the LORD, though I swept you [there] like the four winds of heaven, declares the LORD." Away, escape, O Zion, you who dwell in Fair Babylon! For thus said the LORD of Hosts, He who sent me after glory, concerning the nations that have taken you as spoil: "Whoever touches you touches the pupil of his own eye. For I will lift My hand against them, and they shall be spoil for those they enslaved." Then you shall know that I was sent by the LORD of Hosts.

Zachariah 2:1-13

Those passages speak again about the end of times. In the first verses Zachariah talks about 4 horns that represent the enemies of Israel and as an opposition to them, he talks about 4 smiths who will cut off these horns. These smiths are clearly important figures in the end of times, but who are they?

AND ADONAI SHOWED ME FOUR SMITHS - who are they? Rav Chunah Ben Binz said on behalf of Rabbi Shimon, these four are Mashiach Ben David, Mashiach Ben Yosef, Elias and Mashiach, the righteous priest.

Talmud of Babylon, Tractate Sukkah 52b

According to our sages, in order for us to fit Yeshua as Mashiach, it is necessary to see in him as Ben Yosef and the missions connected to this facet, as well as Ben David and the missions connected to this facet, and also, as a priest through his priestly deeds. To do so, let's look at some specific missions for each facet of the same Mashiach:

-BEN YOSEF
1- TO REDEEM ISRAEL'S LOST TRIBES BY RETURNING THE KNOWLEDGE OF THE TORAH TO THEM.
2- TO REMOVE THE UNCLEAN SPIRIT BY TEACHING HOW TO DEAL WITH THE SPIRITUAL WORLD
3- TO TEACH AND TO REVEAL THE SECRETS OF TORAH

-BEN DAVID
1- TO JUDGE THE NATIONS
2- TO REBUILD JERUSALEM AND THE TEMPLE
3- TO ETERNALLY REIGN

-PRIEST
1- TO ESTABLISH THE SHEKHINAH OF GOD IN THIS REALITY
2- TO BECOME A SACRIFICE
3- TO RESTORE A CONNECTION BETWEEN MEN AND GOD

Apart from the missions described above, the Midrash also establishes some characteristics about all those facets of Mashiach:

1- SAME PERSON, BUT CONNECTED TO SEVERAL TRIBES OF ISRAEL
2- HIS DIFFERENT FACETS WILL BE PRESENTED IN DIFFERENT TIMES
3- MASHIACH BEN DAVID WILL BE A WARRIOR
4- MASHIACH BEN YOSEF WILL BE KILLED
5- MASHIACH BEN YOSEF WILL BE THE FIRST TO RESURRECT

There are some very interesting things about Mashiach throughout rabbinic literature, very interesting accounts that are very clear in Yeshua's deeds:

> *If the Jewish people do not regret, the events of Mashiach Ben Yosef will go unnoticed, but if the people repent, Mashiach Ben David will come suddenly.*

Rabbi Saadiah Gaon

All the prophecy that will be covered in this book will show the connection that Yeshua had, through the fulfillment of these prophecies, with the facet Ben Yosef, Ben David and as a Priest, thus proving what he himself claimed to be, THE MASHIACH, as stipulated by the Tanakh and the Jewish sages.

THE KINGDOM OF ISRAEL

After King Solomon's death around 922 b.c.e., Israel was divided into two parts, the northern kingdom, called the Kingdom of Israel, which encompassed the tribes of Reuven, Dan, Naphtali, Gad, Asher, Issachar, Zevulum, Ephraim and Menasseh, and the southern kingdom, called Yehudah, formed by the tribes of Judah and Benjamin and the Levites circulating between both kingdoms.

In 722 b.c.e., after many warnings from God, the Assyrian empire invaded Israel and the northern kingdom was conquered due to the wickedness of its kings. The vast majority of the people of Israel were exiled, the Assyrian empire displaced almost all the inhabitants of the northern kingdom and dispersed them throughout the known world, most of them were taken to Media and Aram-Naharaim and, in their places, people were brought from several other regions of the empire to live in these lands.

The lost tribes of the Kingdom of Israel is one of the greatest mysteries in Jewish history. Multiple theories have been created on top of that, there are those who say that some are in India, others in Nigeria and there are some others who dare to say that the descendants of these tribes are the native Indians of North America.

Numerous archaeological evidence proves that these people from the Kingdom of Israel were eventually absorbed and assimilated into Gentile societies and therefore, the people of these tribes lost their whereabouts and disappeared completely. Today nobody knows what really happened to them, the only thing left was a prophecy about the descendants of these tribes:

And you, O mortal, take a stick and write on it, "Of Judah and the Israelites associated with him"; and take another stick and write on it, "Of Joseph, the stick of Ephraim and all the House of Israel associated with him." Bring them close to each other, so that they become one stick, joined together in your hand. And when any of your people ask you, "Won't you tell us what these actions of yours mean?" Answer them, "Thus said the Lord GOD: I am going to take the stick of Joseph, which is in the hand of Ephraim, and of the tribes of Israel associated with him, and I will place the stick of Judah upon it and make them into one stick; they shall be joined in My hand."

Ezekiel 37:16-19

Many rabbis teach that in the age of Mashiach, the descendants of these tribes will be reunited in the land of Israel by the hands of the Creator himself. There is something within each individual from the People of Israel that differentiates them from all other nations, apart the Torah, all descendants of Yaakov have a divine spark within their souls, a spark that is passed on from generation to generation. The descendants of these tribes, today spread across the four corners of the world, do not know that they are part of the people once created by God. Many people around the world, from different nationalities and creeds, will be called back through that divine spark that they have within their souls. They will be people who, even without knowing or understanding, will quickly accept this call that will be made through Mashiach.

Rabbi Eliezer says: just as the day is followed by darkness and then the light returns, so too, even if it becomes darkness for the lost tribes, God will definitely bring them out of the darkness.

Talmud of Babylon, Tractate Sanhedrin 110b

The redemptive work of Mashiach is precisely to gather his people, he will bring back all the descendants of Yaakov to serve him. Rabbi Eliezer's statement is a slight allusion that the Talmud makes about Isaiah's prophecy, this rabbinic understanding is the probable reason why Matthew makes a point of quoting Isaiah in his book. The fact that Yeshua had a connection with this region and with some of the people who lived there makes a lot of sense in relation to his claim to be the Mashiach, as this attitude shows, even for a moment and only in a symbolic way, his connection to the Northern Kingdom. When Yeshua went to these regions outside the land of Yehudah, he did not go after Samaritans or Gentiles, nor did he go to do "evangelism", he went after the remnants of these tribes, showing one of his purposes. In one of these travels he states:

> And Yeshua said to them, I was not sent except
> to the lost sheep of the house of Israel.
>
> Matthew 15:24

Many Christians believe that these "Israel's lost sheep" are the Jews who are under the curse of the law or teach that the sheep represent the Gentiles who will accept jesus or even, that these sheep show how the Jewish people are a lost people. But leaving aside all these awful Christian interpretations, this claim shows, in fact, that he came after the lost sheep of the House of Israel, those sheep he refers to are not the Jews, for they are the inhabitants of the House of Yehudah, but rather the lost descendants of the Kingdom of Israel, those people who have been dispersed, lost and belong to the other tribes of Israel. As well as teaching the Torah, redeeming the people and ruling over all nations, another work of Mashiach is precisely to bring together the lost descendants of Yaakov, who was also called Israel. This attitude on the part of Yeshua corroborated with the claim that he makes later on, that he is Mashiach.

The people that walked in darkness Have seen a brilliant light;
On those who dwelt in a land of gloom Light has dawned.

Isaiah 9:1

Another rabbinic commentary about this passage from Isaiah 9 explains more about the end of this dispersion of the lost sheep of Israel:

After the fall of what Assyria did, there will be no
one lost from the House of Israel who will remain
in the dark, for they will see the great light.

Malbim, Isaiah 9:1

In the recent years, a strong approach to the Torah in the Gentile world has taken place. In many parts of the world, many Christians are putting aside the church's common teachings and dogmas to seek answers in the divine Torah. The thirst for knowledge about Adonai grows in the western world in an unprecedented way, many people are forsaking the typical Christian mentality and are associating themselves with the commandments given by God.

Such a phenomenon, as never seen before, tends to grow more and more as the era of Mashiach approaches. Perhaps these people, who abandon religion to assume the yoke of the Torah, are the people who have that divine spark within their souls, the same spark that is found in the children of the tribes of Israel and perhaps, these people are the true descendants of the lost sheep of the house of Israel.

If we make some connections with Yeshua's work, this hypothesis may be plausible, since he himself declares that he came to Israel's lost sheep. Whether one like it or not, it was through his life and death that knowledge about the One God and the Torah reached the Gentiles; And now, 2000 years after his death, one of his mission starts to become clear and concrete, for people are rising and seeking the Torah, because inside their souls, they are being called by Mashiach; Mashiach is calling back his people, those he chose to serve him.

I also believe that it is not because one belongs to any Christian temple or to a Christian branch that he is a descendant of the House of Israel, as many of those who are in these religions are strongly attached to them, to their theories, theologies and dogmas. However, in spite that Christianity chained several people to its dogmas, it was through Christianity itself that God kept these lost sheep close to Him, but now, as the time approaches, the time to separate these people from Western religions and to bring them back to the Creator's true will, there will be more and more people seeking God outsides the religion mindset.

Some say that the signs of the coming of the Mashiach will be perceived by looking at Israel, perhaps this Israel is not the State of Israel, but the Kingdom of Israel. I believe that this spark that exists within many people, which shows that they are the descendants of these lost tribes, will serve as a signal that will precede the coming of Mashiach. This spark will serve as some sort of beacon, because this movement that has been taking place all over the world, where people are increasingly seeking the Torah instead of the teachings of men, clearly shows that God is calling His people for the Messianic era. Perhaps, this is the "Israel" that we must look at, the Gentiles' approach to Israel without any reason and in a miraculous way, placing themselves under the yoke of Torah and under the will of the God of Israel.

GEMATRIA

Gematria is a numerological system by which each of the Hebrew letters correspond to certain numerical values. This system is part of Kabbalah and is a very powerful tool for the interpretation of biblical texts.

Each letter of the Hebrew alphabet is represented by a number. One can then calculate the numerical value of the Hebrew words in the Bible for a more mystical, hidden exegesis of what the Word of God is teaching. In the world of biblical exegesis, many commentators and scholars of the Torah base their arguments on the numerical equivalence of words. When a word has a numerical value equal to another word, there is a mystical connection between them. This shows that both words can be used in both contexts, that is, one can take the place of the other and vice versa, thus revealing an unique understanding of biblical passages.

Many sages believe that Adonai created the universe through the letters of the Hebrew alphabet and therefore, there is a hidden power behind each one. The numbers that each represents serve to hide the Creator's secrets from the common man.

On the other hand, we must be very careful with Gematria, as it is a tool for exclusively biblical use. Making use of it in a secular way, as a means of divination or predictions of the future, is something vehemently prohibited by the Torah and by God. This method has so much power that several pseudo-kabbalists nowadays offer this teaching to lay people for secular use. Other occult sects also know this tool and use it to strengthen their spells and witchcraft. Therefore, I emphasize, Gematria should not be used outside a biblical context and should not be learned through secular books written by unknown authors, nor by people without a direct connection with the divine Torah; it can only be taught and learned by rabbis who use it as a biblical interpretation tool.

Gematria is a tool that I use a lot throughout this book. There are countless ways to use it, in this book I will use some ways as presented in the chart below:

GEMATRIA'S CHART

80	פ/ף	9	ט	1	א
90	צ/ץ	10	י	2	ב
100	ק	20	כ/ך	3	ג
200	ר	30	ל	4	ד
300	ש	40	מ/ם	5	ה
400	ת	50	נ/ן	6	ו
		60	ס	7	ז
		70	ע	8	ח

Absolute Value

17	פ/ף	9	ט	1	א
18	צ/ץ	10	י	2	ב
19	ק	11	כ/ך	3	ג
20	ר	12	ל	4	ד
21	ש	13	מ/ם	5	ה
22	ת	14	נ/ן	6	ו
		15	ס	7	ז
		16	ע	8	ח

Mispar Siduri

8	פ/ף	9	ט	1	א
9	צ/ץ	1	י	2	ב
1	ק	2	כ/ך	3	ג
2	ר	3	ל	4	ד
3	ש	4	מ/ם	5	ה
4	ת	5	נ/ן	6	ו
		6	ס	7	ז
		7	ע	8	ח

Mispar Katan

6	פ/ף	50	ט	400	א
5	צ/ץ	40	י	300	ב
4	ק	30	כ/ך	200	ג
3	ר	20	ל	100	ד
2	ש	10	מ/ם	90	ה
1	ת	9	נ/ן	80	ו
		8	ס	70	ז
		7	ע	60	ח

EtBash

100	ק	10	י	1	א
200	ר	20	כ	2	ב
300	ש	30	ל	3	ג
400	ת	40	מ	4	ד
500	ך	50	נ	5	ה
600	ם	60	ס	6	ו
700	ן	70	ע	7	ז
800	ף	80	פ	8	ח
900	ץ	90	צ	9	ט

Absolute Value with Sofit

TERMINOLOGY

For those who do not know the Hebrew language or are not used to rabbinic terminology, it is vitally important that the following terms are studied and understood before reading this book:

Torah - The first five books of the bible - Genesis, Exodus, Leviticus, Numbers, Deuteronomy - also known as the Law of Moses. The Torah is the most holy of all books, as it is the only one that reveals the true "ME" of the Creator of all things.

Mishnah - It is the other name for the Oral Torah, it addresses all the commandments of the Torah.

Gemarah - These are the rabbinic commentaries on the Mishnah. It is also known as the Talmud, and they have numerous laws created by the sages and imposed on the Jewish people.

Midrash - Commentaries from the sages on biblical passages, the Midrashim were composed in Aramaic and have an unparalleled wisdom.

Talmud - Mishnah + Gemarah + some external teachings.

Tzadik - This is a vital term for understanding Yeshua's words. A TZADIK is a person who observes and obeys the Laws of the Torah. This term is commonly translated as "righteous" and due to that, it lost all its essence. Being a Tzadik is the life goal of any Jew who loves God.

Tanakh - Torah + Prophets + Writings = Hebrew Bible or Old Testament.

Mitzvah (Mitzvot, plural) - Commandments of the Torah.

Parashah - The Torah is divided into 54 portions called parashah, for a complete reading in a one-year cycle.

ALL THE PASSAGES FROM THE TANAKH, MIDRASHIM, TALMUD AND THE RABBINIC COMMENTARIES USED IN THIS BOOK WERE TRANSLATED FROM THEIR ORIGINAL LANGUAGES (HEBREW OR ARAMAIC) BY THE AUTHOR OF THIS BOOK, UNLESS IDENTIFIED THE TRANSLATION USED. FOR THAT REASON, THESE PASSAGES MAY PRESENT SOME DIFFERENCES WHEN COMPARED TO THE MOST COMMON WESTERN TRANSLATIONS.

MANY VERSES FROM THE TANAKH DO NOT HAVE

THE SAME NUMBERING THAT THE OLD TESTAMENT'S TRANSLATION HAS, THEREFORE THERE WILL BE SOME DIFFERENCES IN THE NUMBERING OF SOME VERSES.

THE PASSAGES USED FROM THE BOOK OF MATTHEW IN THIS BOOK, ARE FROM THE TRANSLATION MADE BY THIS AUTHOR FROM THE ORIGINAL HEBREW BOOK OF MATTHEW.

Remove all false ways from me; favor me with Your teaching.
Psalms 119:29

THE NAME IN
THE PROPHECY

מֵעֹצֶר וּמִמִּשְׁפָּט לֻקָּח וְאֶת־דּוֹרוֹ מִי יְשׂוֹחֵחַ כִּי נִגְזַר מֵאֶרֶץ חַיִּים מִפֶּשַׁע עַמִּי נֶגַע לָמוֹ
וַיִּתֵּן אֶת־רְשָׁעִים קִבְרוֹ וְאֶת־עָשִׁיר בְּמֹתָיו עַל לֹא־חָמָס עָשָׂה וְלֹא מִרְמָה בְּפִיו
וַיהֹוָה חָפֵץ דַּכְּאוֹ הֶחֱלִי אִם־תָּשִׂים אָשָׁם נַפְשׁוֹ יִרְאֶה
זֶרַע יַאֲרִיךְ יָמִים וְחֵפֶץ יְהוָה בְּיָדוֹ יִצְלָח

By oppressive judgment he was taken away, Who could describe his abode? For he was cut off from the land of the living Through the sin of my people, who deserved the punishment. And his grave was set among the wicked, And with the rich, in his death, Though he had done no injustice And had spoken no falsehood. But the LORD chose to crush him by disease, That, if he made himself an offering for guilt, He might see offspring and have long life, And that through him the LORD's purpose might prosper in his hand.
Isaiah 53:8-10

Unfortunately, many of those who believe in Yeshua, do also believe that his name is jesus, among those who know that his name is really Yeshua, there are also those who believe that there is no difference between treating him by his real name or by the name jesus.

There are some revelations that are inevitably lost when we do not read the bible in its original language. One of them is the word pun used by the angel when he told Yosef what his son's name should be, I'll put the verse in it's original language and I will leave two terms in their original form:

And she shall give birth to a son and he will be called
YESHUA, *for* **YOSHIA** *my people from their iniquities.*

Matthew 1:21

Here we see something very common in Hebrew texts, this type of word pun appears in numerous passages throughout the Tanakh and in the Talmud. This is a further proof that the book of Matthew was originally written in Hebrew. YOSHIA means "He Will Save", as it appears in Western translations, but the biggest problem here is that we have the impression that the one who is going to save is jesus, or Yeshua, and here is where the problem lies when one does not understand his true name. Yeshua is a variant of the name Yehoshua, just like the name Daniel stands Dani or the name Thomas stands Tom. There are reports of this variant in the Tanakh:

The Israelites had not done so since the days
of **Yeshua** *Ben Nun to this day.*

Nehemiah 8:17

Then **Yeshua**, *the son of Yozadak ...*

Ezra 3:2a

The Yeshua in the book of Ezra was the high priest at the time of the construction of the second temple, if we look in the English translation, his name will be presented as Joshua. Just as in the first verse above, Yeshua Ben Nun is none other than Joshua, Moses' servant, who led the people into the promised land. That is, in English, the name of jesus is Joshua, for Joshua in Hebrew is Yeshua, a "nickname" from the name Yehoshua. It is worth remembering that this is not the original name of Joshua, his name was Hoshea, but it was changed by God at a certain point in his life, just as it happened with Abraham, Sarah and Yaakov.

Now that we know what his real name is, we must find out what weight that name has and what it can reveal to us about his own mission.

Yehoshua is a junction of a name and a verb, as well as the name Rafael (Rafa - heals + EL - God). The name that is used in in the word Yehoshua is precisely THE NAME ABOVE ALL NAMES, the Tetragram (יהוה) – *YEHOxxx* – in connection with the verb LEHOSHIA (להושיע) – *to save* - conjugated in the in the future tense of the third-person of singular YOSHIA (יושע).

YEHOxxx (**יהו**) + yoSHIA (יו**שע**) = YEHOSHUA (יהושע)

The name Yehoshua is the junction of the true and deepest name of the Creator to the verb "to save" in the future form. So, in this way, we have ADONAI WILL SAVE, unlike the word jesus, which means nothing. In the book of Matthew, his name appears in the contracted form of Yeshua, but in other books in its originals versions, such as the book of Luke and the book of Yohanan, his full name appears as Yehoshua Ben Yosef. As mentioned above, people called Yehoshua ended up receiving the "nickname" of Yeshua, something very customary until the first century.

Interesting fact

The famous modern rabbi Yitzhak Kaduri, who died in 2007 at the age of 106, was a famous religious master in Israel, considered one of the greatest connoisseurs of Jewish mysticism and a strong influencer on political and social causes of the State of Israel. Rabbi Kaduri was considered the supreme authority of Kabbalah and his predictions were very accurate, his prophecies were always seen as warnings and his counsels as true blessings.

A few months before his death, Rabbi Kaduri wrote the name of Mashiach on a small piece of paper as revealed to him by God and asked that it only be opened seven months after his death. According to the Israel Today newspaper, the note reads as follows:

As for the letters of the abbreviation of the
name of Mashiach, he will raise the people and
prove that his words and laws are true.

This one I signed in the month of chessed,
Yitzhak Kaduri

Many were disappointed at first with this note, for they were waiting for the revelation of the name of Mashiach, and it was at that moment that they realized something which is only possible to see by the way it was written in Hebrew:

ירים **ה**עם **ו**יוכיח **ש**דברו **ו**תורתו **ע**ומדים

Yarim HaAm VeYokhiah SheDbaro VeTorato Omdim

From right to left, if we get the first letters of each word we will have (יהושוע), transliterating, YEHOSHUA.

I firmly believe that the name of Mashiach that will rule over all nations is Yehoshua, and I say this because of the many missions Mashiach will have, one of them is the restoration of Jerusalem and its Temple.

Such feats will not be exclusive to Mashiach, since two other people have already done so. One of them was Ezra, who rebuilt the Temple that was destroyed by the Babylonians and the second one was Nehemiah, when he rebuilt the walls of Jerusalem, which in an indirect way, represents the restoration of the City. But the question is, what does all of this have to do with the name Yehoshua? Well, Everything!

If we make a mystical analysis of their names using Gematria, many things can be revealed and we will be able to see something very deep.

NEHEMIAH (נחמיה)

נ50 + ח8 + מ40 + י10 + ה5

= **113**

ESDRAS (עזרא)

ע70 + ז7 + ר200 + א1

= **278**

YEHOSHUA (יהושע)

ע70 + ש300 + ו6 + ה5 + י10

= **391**

Well, we have the value for the name of Ezra of 278, Nehemiah's of 113, and Yehoshua's of 391. Apparently there is no connection between the three, but if we think that Nehemiah rebuilt the wall and the city, Ezra rebuilt the Temple and Yehoshua will do the work of both of them by restoring the city and the Temple, we would have:

278 (Ezra) + **113** (Nehemiah) = **391** (Yehoshua)

Now we have another proof that the name of Mashiach is Yehoshua, for as Ezra and Nehemiah rebuilt the wall, the city and the Temple, Mashiach will restore the holy city, will protected it and will rebuild the Holy Temple. The name Yehoshua shows that Mashiach will bring the revelation of the Living God and His Torah, by which, Adonai will save. It also shows his mission to rebuild the holy city and the Temple and finally, as Joshua (also Yehoshua) led the people to the land of Israel, Mashiach will also lead his people back to the holy land.

To know the true name of Mashiach makes all the difference.

May Hashem grant us the gift of being able to study
and to teach for all the days of our lives, so that we
have the merit of the final redemption, when Mashiach
Ben David comes to rebuild the Temple.
Rav. Moshe Feinstein, Iggeros Moshe, V I 17

The definitive result will be when Mashiach comes and
the Holy City will descend from the heavens.

Kav HaYashar 102

He will bring Israel from all parts to his holy city, the nation that will build His Temple. The TZADIK will gather around Mashiach and those who study the Torah will be able to study it with him.
Metsudah Chumash, Bereshit 49:11

Now, returning to the prophetic verse in question, Isaiah chapter 53, the prophet speaks about the suffering and death that Mashiach Ben Yosef would have to go through, a prophecy that fits very well with the accounts of Yeshua's life. However, this is not the main point in this study, but rather his name. For this reason, we should look back at those verses with different eyes.

מֵעֹצֶר וּמִמִּשְׁפָּט לֻקָּח וְאֶת־דּוֹרוֹ מִי יְשׂוֹחֵחַ כִּי נִגְזַר מֵאֶרֶץ חַיִּים מִפֶּשַׁע עַמִּי נֶגַע לָמוֹ

וַיִּתֵּן אֶת־רְשָׁעִים קִבְרוֹ וְאֶת־עָשִׁיר בְּמֹתָיו עַל לֹא־חָמָס עָשָׂה וְלֹא מִרְמָה בְּפִיו

וַיהוָה חָפֵץ דַּכְּאוֹ הֶחֱלִי אִם־תָּשִׂים אָשָׁם נַפְשׁוֹ יִרְאֶה

זֶרַע יַאֲרִיךְ יָמִים וְחֵפֶץ יְהוָה בְּיָדוֹ יִצְלָח

Isaiah 53:7-10

Looking back at these three verses in their original language, starting from the letter YUD (י) of the word (יאריך), as highlighted above, and with a count of every 20 letters starting with the last verse and from left to right, after the first letter YUD (י) we have the letters SHIN (ש), VAV (ו), AYN (ע), SHIN (ש), MEM (מ) and again the letter YUD (י).

This forms the word YESHUA SHMI (ישוע שמי), which means YESHUA IS MY NAME!

Here is another striking revelation about the name of Mashiach and how mystically the Tanakh already revealed something about Yeshua. Some sages, through deep divine revelation, already have this understanding that can be seen in the following prophetic Psalm:

> *May his name be eternal; while the sun lasts, may*
> *YNNON endure; let men invoke his blessedness upon*
> *themselves; let all nations count him happy.*
>
> Psalms 72:17

> *About Mashiach, Gemarah asks: What's his name? Rabbi*
> *Yannai's school says: YNNON is his name, for it is written: May*
> *his name be eternal, may his name exist as long as the sun.*
>
> Talmud of Babylon, Tractate Sanhedrin 98b

According to Rabbi Yannai's School, Mashiach's name is YNNON. This name, although seems strange, is a Cabalistic name to refer to the name Yeshua, for by Gematria we have the following:

YESHUA (ישוע)

7ע + 6ו + 3ש + 1י

= **17**

YNNON (יננו)

5ן + 6ו + 5נ + 1י

= **17**

Both YESHUA and YNNON have the same numerical value (17) as it is a coded way to refer to him.

From all of the above, you can see the importance of the name of Mashiach. Those who cling to other words to deal with Yeshua's name, completely lose the essence that his name possesses and inevitably end up serving a mythical being, thus entering into idolatry.

Blessed are those who understand these things.

BEN YOSEF

נִבְזֶה וַחֲדַל אִישִׁים אִישׁ מַכְאֹבוֹת וִידוּעַ חֹלִי וּכְמַסְתֵּר פָּנִים מִמֶּנּוּ נִבְזֶה וְלֹא חֲשַׁבְנֻהוּ

אָכֵן חֳלָיֵנוּ הוּא נָשָׂא וּמַכְאֹבֵינוּ סְבָלָם וַאֲנַחְנוּ חֲשַׁבְנֻהוּ נָגוּעַ מֻכֵּה אֱלֹהִים וּמְעֻנֶּה

וְהוּא מְחֹלָל מִפְּשָׁעֵנוּ מְדֻכָּא מֵעֲוֹנֹתֵינוּ מוּסַר שְׁלוֹמֵנוּ עָלָיו וּבַחֲבֻרָתוֹ נִרְפָּא־לָנוּ

כֻּלָּנוּ כַּצֹּאן תָּעִינוּ אִישׁ לְדַרְכּוֹ פָּנִינוּ וַיהוָה הִפְגִּיעַ בּוֹ אֵת עֲוֹן כֻּלָּנוּ

נִגַּשׂ וְהוּא נַעֲנֶה וְלֹא יִפְתַּח־פִּיו כַּשֶּׂה לַטֶּבַח יוּבָל וּכְרָחֵל לִפְנֵי גֹזְזֶיהָ נֶאֱלָמָה וְלֹא יִפְתַּח פִּיו

מֵעֹצֶר וּמִמִּשְׁפָּט לֻקָּח וְאֶת־דּוֹרוֹ מִי יְשׂוֹחֵחַ כִּי נִגְזַר מֵאֶרֶץ חַיִּים מִפֶּשַׁע עַמִּי נֶגַע לָמוֹ

He was despised, shunned by men, A man of suffering, familiar with disease. As one who hid his face from us, He was despised, we held him of no account. Yet it was our sickness that he was bearing, Our suffering that he endured. We accounted him plagued, Smitten and afflicted by God; But he was wounded because of our sins, Crushed because of our iniquities. He bore the chastisement that made us whole, And by his bruises we were healed. We all went astray like sheep, Each going his own way; And the LORD visited upon him The guilt of all of us." He was maltreated, yet he was submissive, He did not open his mouth; Like a sheep being led to slaughter, Like a ewe, dumb before those who shear her, He did not open his mouth. By oppressive judgment he was taken away, Who could describe his abode? For he was cut off from the land of the living Through the sin of my people, who deserved the punishment.

Isaiah 53:3-8

But Yeshua answered not a word. The high priest said to him, I adjure you by the living EL, that you

tell us if you are the Mashiach, the son of EL.

Matthew 26:63

These passages from the book of the prophet Isaiah, when compared to everything the gospel tells us, are easily understood. The life, death, and all the suffering that Yeshua endured fit quite well with the words from the verses above, since they took place in his life. However, if we look at those prophecies in a little more spiritual manner, we shall see that they are not just dealing with the suffering he has had to go through, but rather they are dealing with one of his facet of Mashiach, for Isaiah is stealthily talking about the three main missions he has.

Before we go any deeper, we must first look into some basic concepts, little known by Christianity, about the true facet of Mashiach.

TWO MASHIACHIM

Our sages teach that there will be two Mashiachim, one known as Mashiach Ben Yosef and the second Mashiach Ben David. In fact, Ben Yosef and Ben David do not represent two people, but two distinct missions that will be performed by only one Mashiach.

The Oral Torah has several Tractates that deal with this belief, let's look at a few:

Rabbi Ben Dosa says: The earth will mourn about the Mashiach that will be murdered... ...This explains that the reason for this is the murder of Mashiach Ben Yosef.

Talmud of Babylon, Tractate Sukkah 52a

The beginning of the war of Gog and Magog will happen with the coming of Mashiach Ben David.

Kol HaTor 1:14

Mashiach Ben Yosef will be the first representation of Mashiach and as reported by the sages, he will be murdered by men.

According to an archaeological finding called *"stone manuscript of the dead sea"*, dated about 110 years before Yeshua's birth, says that Mashiach Ben Yosef, after his death, would resuscitate. In the other hand, Mashiach Ben David will have the mission to rule over the entire world, to defeat his enemies, to restore the Temple and he will establish a thousand years reign. Those are the two facets of the same Mashiach, facets established according to different missions and time in human's history.

Mission of Mashiach

For a better understanding about Mashiach, knowing his mission is essential.

> *The earthly mission of Mashiach Ben Yosef has three fronts: revelation of the mysteries of the Torah, to return the exiled and to remove the unclean spirit from the earth.*
> Kol HaTor 1:11

1- TO REMOVE THE UNCLEAN SPIRIT

> *I will see him, but not now; I will contemplate him, but not now. A star shall come from Yaakov, and a scepter shall ascend out of Israel, which shall smite the Moabites, and shall destroy all the sons of Seth.*
> Numbers 24:17

In this passage we have words uttered by the prophet Bil'am, a prophet who came to prophesy against the People of Israel while they were in the desert; the words that came out from the mouth of this man are extremely mystical and full of hidden messages.

By mentioning Yaakov, it is prophesied that a star will come from him, the name of Yaakov was changed to Israel, so, we can understand that this "star" will come from Israel, a star that certainly represents Mashiach.

The second thing concerns Mashiach's origin, for the term

"shall smite the Moabites", is the same term that appears in II Samuel 8:2, when it is reported that King David "smote the Moabites", using exactly the same Hebrew terms. With this, we can make a connection of this star, that comes from Israel, with king David.

Lastly, it will be his final mission to destroy Seth's sons. Seth, as son of Adam, begat all nations, so the term "sons of Seth" refers to the nations that do not recognize and do not follow the God of Israel. Mashiach will have no mercy upon them, he will not come to preach to such people, he will not come to teach them to repent, but he will come to destroy all the nations which are God's enemies. And that is the meaning of "to remove the unclean spirit from the earth", it is to remove their pagan believes.

> *At that time Yeshua said to his talmidim, do not think that I came to put in the nations (peace), but rather desolation.*
> Matthew 10:34

Indeed, the concept "jesus" by it self already brought much war and death between nations and peoples. But the term "desolation" which he uses, a term that was erroneously translated as "sword" in English, in its original language, we have the term *HaShkutz Shomem*, this is the same term that appears in the book of Daniel, a term that can be translated as "Abomination of Desolation". This weird term is commonly used to refer to idolatry and to the pagan nations. Idolatry is the lowest level of impurity and the most hated thing by God.

What Yeshua is actually saying in this verse is that he will cause the Abomination of Desolation, as seen in the book of Daniel, but in the way he expresses himself in Hebrew, one must understand that he will impose himself against the nations that practice idolatry, thus removing all uncleanness by destroying them, alongside with their practices and believers.

2- TO TEACH TORAH

As the definition about the deeds of Mashiach is strongly approached by the Oral Torah, it is for it that we should look at in order to understand some things:

> *(Gen 41:45) "He who explains what is hidden" - This was said about Yosef, and it is one of the missions of Mashiach Ben Yosef, for he will reveal the hidden secrets of the Torah for all generations.*
>
> Kol HaTor 2:122

One of the main missions of Mashiach is to teach the Torah and this is of the utmost importance. The sages say that all the other books of the Scriptures will become just historical books, for the only one that will remain valid as "bible" is the Torah itself, this is because of Mashiach's explanation as to how it should be lived, leaving aside the need for prophets and sages.

Yeshua, in order to be seen as Mashiach, in addition to never being able to abolish the Torah, he must concentrate 100% of his teachings on its commandments and teachings, as well as how they should be observed and lived; this is one of the main missions of Mashiach.

> *Take my yoke as your yoke and learn from my Torah, for I am humble, I am good and pure in heart and you will find rest in your souls.*
>
> Matthew 11:29

Self-explanatory passage, Yeshua is very clear in saying "my Torah", i.e. "my interpretation of Torah". It is the way he understands it, how he teaches it and how he reveals it to the world.

I would like to make a brief analysis of the term yoke, as it gives the impression of something negative. In rabbinic language, when a student comes under the supervision of a rabbi, that student is said to have taken the yoke of that master. The yoke is nothing more than a wood made clapboard used upon the necks of two oxen in order to make them walk side by side. The term yoke was not used as a burden on one's shoulders, but rather as something that makes two people walk side by side, just as any student's intentions should be to walk side by side with his teacher.

Yeshua, by using this term, calls people to walk side by side with him according to his interpretation of Torah, that is, according to his own *halachah.*

3- TO RETURN THE EXILED
This is a well known prophecy, repeated in many parts throughout the Tanakh, the return of the Jewish people to the land of Israel today is a reality after nearly two thousand years.

> *Then Adonai, your God will restore your fortunes and take you back in love. He will gather you again from all the nations where Adonai your God will spread you.*
> Deuteronomy 30:3

The sages say that the first verses of Deuteronomy 30 refers precisely to Mashiach and his deeds. Verse 3 deals exactly with the great work of God to bring His people back to the land of Israel.

Yeshua, as a great connoisseur of rabbinical teachings, knew about this three missions expected from Mashiach very well, especially about his mission to bring back the people from the Kingdom of Israel, and for this reason, he made an interesting comment about it:

> *And Yeshua said to them, I was not sent except to the lost sheep of the house of Israel.*
> Matthew 15:24

Many Christian preachings state that, in this verse, Yeshua referred to the sinners of Israel, that he came to forgive and to teach them. However, the term Beit Israel (House of Israel) as used in this verse, is commonly used by Gemarah to refer to the northern kingdom, known as the Kingdom of Israel, which was invaded by the Assyrians and had its people dispersed and assimilated throughout the world.

So, what Yeshua teaches here is one of his main missions; he says that Mashiach will rescue these people and will reunite them as God's people, as the true Israel. Some sages say that the non-Jew who accepts the yoke of the Torah out of the blue is somehow descended from these people who have been scattered throughout the world and has a sparkle inside of him, a sparkle that differentiates them from the others nations and makes them God's chosen people, even if they do not know it.

ISAIAH'S PROPHECY AND MASHIACH'S MISSION

Returning to the words of the prophet, we can find these three Mashiach Ben Yosef's missions in Isaiah's prophecies. If we look at some verses from chapter 53 of the book of Isaiah in a little more mystical way, we shall see that he addresses these three missions in a very interesting way, for through those words of Isaiah, the author of the book of Matthew were able to state that those missions were fulfilled by Yeshua.

> *But he was wounded because of our sins, Crushed because of our iniquities. He bore the chastisement that made us whole, And by his bruises we were healed.*
>
> Isaiah 53:5

The verse 5, by Gematria's calculation, we will have a total sum of 3264 of its letters. This numerical value is the same total value found in the following Torah passages:

> *Pharaoh then summoned Moses and said, "Go, worship the LORD! Only your flocks and your herds shall be left behind; even your children may go with you."*
>
> Exodus 10:24

*On the third new moon after the Israelites had
gone forth from the land of Egypt, on that very
day, they entered the wilderness of Sinai.*

Exodus 19:1

From the Torah passages that are strikingly connected with Isaiah chapter 53 verse 5, we see the same theme being addressed in both of them; the freedom of the Hebrews and their formation as a people before the eyes of the Creator.

Both speak about freedom, the departure of foreign lands, the break up with paganism and the gathering of all as one people. This is amazing, for those deeds are directly connected with one of the missions of Mashiach Ben Yosef as seen above, the return of His people from foreign lands, from pagan cultures and from mentalities far from the will of the true God.

*We all went astray like sheep, Each going his own way; And
the LORD visited upon him The guilt of all of us."*

Isaiah 53:6

In the next verse, by Gematria, we have a total numerical value of 2411 of it letters, which is exactly the same as a passage found in the book of Deuteronomy:

*The Torah, taught us by Moses, to the heritage
of the congregation of Yaakov.*

Deuteronomy 33:4

Amazingly, now we have the connection related to Mashiach Ben Yosef's second mission, the teaching of the Torah. The above verse is quite straightforward when quoting TORAH, TEACH, and YAAKOV, which was later called ISRAEL. This reveals to us what was the basis of Yeshua's ministry, the teaching and the true interpretation of the Torah to all who are part of (and also grafted into) the People of Israel.

By oppressive judgment he was taken away, Who could describe

his abode? For he was cut off from the land of the living
Through the sin of my people, who deserved the punishment.

Isaiah 53:8

Lastly, Gematria's total sum of verse 8 is 3516. This numerical value connects this verse to another very interesting Torah's passage:

For I the LORD am He who brought you up from the land of
Egypt to be your God: **you shall be holy, for I am holy**.

Leviticus 11:45

Holiness is only achievable when one's life is according to the will of the Creator and His commandments. The commandments does not only bring man close to God, but also make him sinless, thus making him clean and holy.

Thus we see that, through Mashiach's Torah interpretation, a holy life is attainable, a life far from impurities and sins, and so, we have the removal of the unclean spirit in the life of the man who understands those things. When Mashiach's Torah is followed by all men, then, consequently, the unclean spirit will be removed from our midst and with that, we learn the third mission of Mashiach Ben Yosef.

The Isaiah prophecy of chapter 53, besides being a direct prophecy about what Yeshua would suffer, it also has a hidden aspect; it reveals to us the true messianic identity of Yeshua through Mashiach's three most important missions that were accomplished by him. By this, we understand that Isaiah spoke about Ben Yosef, about the first representation of Mashiach in our reality.

This prophecy, as all other prophecies, must be understood beyond the prophesied suffering that he would undergo, for they reveal us the true Yeshua Ben Yosef, a Mashiach not understood by most of his so called "followers".

◆ ◆ ◆

THE VIRGIN

לָכֵן יִתֵּן אֲדֹנָי הוּא לָכֶם אוֹת הִנֵּה הָעַלְמָה הָרָה וְיֹלֶדֶת בֵּן וְקָרָאת שְׁמוֹ עִמָּנוּ אֵל

Assuredly, my Lord will give you a sign of His own accord!
Look, the young woman is with child and about to give
birth to a son. Let her name him Ym'Anu'El.

Isaiah 7:14

The birth of Yeshua was in this way) It came to pass when his
mother was betrothed to Yosef, before he knew her, she was found
pregnant by the Holy Spirit. Yosef was a Tzadik man and did not
wish to live with her nor to expose her by bringing her to shame or
to bind her over to death. Instead, he concealed her. While he thought
on this matter in his heart, an angel came to him in a dream and
said, Yosef, son of David, do not fear to take your wife Miriam,
because she is pregnant by the Holy Spirit. And she will give birth to a
son and he will be called Yeshua, for he will save my people from their
iniquities. All this was to fulfill what was written by the prophet
according to Adonai. The young woman is conceiving and will bear
a son and you will call him Ym'Anu'El, that is, Elohim is with us.

Matthew 1:18-23

My intention is not to explain the miracle of a birth without
the paternal seed, but to explain the reasons for this. Such a
fact is such a profound miracle that, throughout many studies, it is normal a little disregard for why such a miracle occurred.

What I want to propose here are the reasons why God decided
to do so. Certainly, it was not because God is the only father
of Yeshua, but rather it was for a much deeper spiritual reason

that the human mind cannot conceive by itself. The study I propose here is not intended to explain how God acts, but what this particular action can teach us about Yeshua and what this miraculous conception teaches us about his person.

THE PATERNAL SEED

Within the Jewish Halachah, what defines an individual as Jewish is the womb that gave birth to him, if the mother is Jewish, the children are Jewish, regardless of whether or not the father is Jewish; The same does not apply if only the father is Jewish, if so the children are not Jewish. On the other hand, the paternal seed is what defines the tribe to which the child belongs. The father passes on to his descendants the tribe and his lineage and the mother passes on Judaism and her lineage.

When the New Testament states that Yeshua was born of a Jewish woman, descendant of David, it automatically states that Yeshua is a Jew, of David's lineage and so belonging to the Kingdom of Judah (kingdom, not tribe). Because he received no paternal seed, and although Joseph is from the tribe of Judah, Yeshua is not legally part of this tribe; however, he is associated with it by *Jus Solis,* that is, a Jew who was born in the territory of that tribe.

God does not backpedal on his ordinances. If Yeshua had received a paternal seed from Judah, he might well have been Mashiach Ben David and able to become legally king, but he could not have become a sacrifice, for he would not belong to the tribe of Levi and his mission would have lost most its meaning; and there would also been two Mashiach, for Mashiach Ben Yosef is linked to the tribe of Efrayim and not Judah. With a little common sense, it is clear why Yeshua came without receiving a paternal seed, without a direct spiritual association with any specific tribe, for he represents three tribes, Efrayim as Ben Yosef, Levi as priest, and Judah as Ben David, and for being of David's lineage on the maternal side and citizen of the tribe of Judah, he is entitled to the royal throne.

The verse above of Isaiah, which presents us the prophecy about the conception of Yeshua, has a total value of 3306 when its letters are summed by Gematria. Throughout the Tanakh, there are three other verses that have exactly the same value, they are *Ezekiel 21:30*, *Ezekiel 38:14* and *Exodus 12:9*.

These three verses have all the answers we need to understand the reasons why God performed the miracle of a virgin birth and also, three essential characteristics about the person and the mission of Yeshua.

EFRAYIM

וְאַתָּה חָלָל רָשָׁע נְשִׂיא יִשְׂרָאֵל אֲשֶׁר־בָּא יוֹמוֹ בְּעֵת עֲוֺן קֵץ

And to you, O dishonored wicked prince of Israel, whose day has come, the time set for your punishment.

Ezequiel 21:30

The first passage of our study talks about the Kingdom of Israel that would be destroyed due to the disobedience of its leaders and the scattering of the people of that kingdom, something that has already been talked about in this book. After Assyria invaded these lands and dispersed its inhabitants throughout the known world, all that remained was ruins, as God reveals two verses later:

עַוָּה עַוָּה עַוָּה אֲשִׂימֶנָּה גַּם־זֹאת לֹא הָיָה עַד־בֹּא אֲשֶׁר־לוֹ הַמִּשְׁפָּט וּנְתַתִּיו

Ruin, an utter ruin I will make it. It shall be no more until he comes to whom it rightfully belongs; and I will give it to him.

Ezequiel 21:32

The people of Israel are directly linked to Ben Yosef, for they represent one of his main missions. According to verse 32, God says that everything will be ruined until the one, to whom it rightfully belongs, comes, and this one is certainly Mashiach. That is, God is saying that the people of the kingdom of Israel, and its descendants, will be in ruins until Mashiach comes and also, this people will be given to him by God Himself. For this reason, as we are talking about the Kingdom of Israel, it is inevitable not to associate this verse with the facet of Ben Yosef.

By Gematria, the number that represents Mashiach Ben Yosef is the number 8, as follows:

MASHIACH BEN YOSEF (משיח בן יוסף)

8ף + 60 + 6י + 1' + 5ן + 2ב + 8ח + 1' + 3ש + 4מ

= 44 = 4+4 = **8**

Returning to the verse of Ezekiel that speaks about Mashiach; from left to right, from the last letter MEM (מ) of this verse (as highlighted below), the EIGHTH (**8**x1) letter is the letter BET (ב) and the SIXTEENTH (**8**x2) letter from the letter Bet is the letter YUD ('), as follows:

עַוָּה עַוָּה עַוָּה אֲשִׂ**י**מֶנָּה גַּם־זֹאת לֹא הָיָה עַד־**בָּ**א אֲשֶׁר־לֹו הַ**מִּ**שְׁפָּט וּנְתַתִּיו

Ezequiel 21:32

Those are the initials of:

מ - משיח (Mashiach)

ב - בן (Ben)

י - יוסף (Yosef)

The first revelation that we have about the prophecy of the conception of Yeshua is that he is Mashiach Ben Yosef, the one who came to teach the Torah, to cast out the unclean spirit, and to seek the descendants of Israel who are scattered throughout the nations of the world. This also teaches us why Yeshua had no earthly father, for Ben Yosef is linked to the tribe of Efrayim and since Yeshua has no tribe by the laws of the Torah, he has the authority to associate himself with the twelve tribes of Israel, which makes him a Mashiach even more connected with the People of God.

Mashiach Ben Yosef associates with Efrayim, as
when he said "Efrayim is My firstborn".

Rabbi Gaon of Vilna

But is Yeshua the name of Ben Yosef?

YESHUA (ישוע)

7ע + 6ו + 3ש + 1י

$17 = 1+7 = \mathbf{8}$

Just as MASHIACH BEN YOSEF is 8, so is YESHUA. Therefore, Yeshua, just like Ben Yosef, associate themselves with the tribe of Efrayim and this is proven by the value that represents THE TRIBE OF EFRAYIM:

HASHEVET EFRAYIM (השבט אפרים) - THE TRIBE OF EFRAYIM

40ם + 10י + 200ר + 80פ + 1א + 9ט + 2ב + 300ש + 5ה

$= 647 = 6+4+7 = 17 = 1+7 = \mathbf{8}$

The kingdom of Israel, the lost tribes, are in the hands of Mashiach Ben Yosef, this is his mission. It is to this facet of Mashiach that this people rightfully belong, a people which is scattered and lost among the nations and are now being called back thanks to the death of Yeshua, which has taken the Torah to the four corners of the earth, so that it may reach and bring this people back together under the wings of God.

YEHUDAH

לָכֵן הִנָּבֵא בֶן־אָדָם וְאָמַרְתָּ לְגוֹג כֹּה אָמַר אֲדֹנָי יְהוִה הֲלוֹא
בַּיּוֹם הַהוּא בְּשֶׁבֶת עַמִּי יִשְׂרָאֵל לָבֶטַח תֵּדָע |

Therefore prophesy, O mortal, and say to Gog: Thus
said the Lord GOD: Surely, on that day, when My people
Israel are living secure, you will take note.

Ezekiel 38:14

This is one of the verses that has the same value as Isaiah 7:14. In it we see God commanding the prophet Ezekiel to prophesy against Gog. Both Gog and Magog appear in some parts of the Tanakh, such as in Genesis, in Ezekiel, and in the book of Revelations. In some parts they are referred to as leaders, or princes, but mostly, they refer to two regions also known as Meshech and Tubal.

Gog and Magog are automatically associated with the "Gog and Magog War", a moment yet to come when the nations of the world, especially the Christians, will come together to make war against Israel. This is a long-awaited war in Judaism, especially among the most orthodox jews, for it is when Mashiach Ben David will come and will triumph, establishing his eternal reign of peace where all nations will be subdued under his authority. Amazingly, it is very possible that the only ones who will stand by Israel's side will be their brothers, the Arab nations, as prophecies concerning Gog and Magog also appear in the Quran.

> *The beginning of the war of Gog and Magog will begin*
> *with the coming of Mashiach Ben David.*
>
> Kol HaTor 1:14

Thus, it is clear that this prophecy concerning Gog has a connection with Mashiach Ben David, which is one of the facets of Mashiach, the facet that has the mission of winning this war and reigning over the whole world from a Jerusalem that will be spiritually restored with the building the third Temple. By Gematria, it is possible to make several calculations upon Mashiach Ben David, one of them is known as Mispar Gadol and it is through it that we must begin:

MASHIACH BEN DAVID (משיח בן דויד)
4ד + 10י + 6ו + 4ד + 700ן + 2ב + 8ח + 10י + 300ש + 40מ
= 1084 = 1+0+8+4 = **4**

The number 4 is not the number directly connected with Mashiach Ben David, for his spiritual number is 10. However, the number 4 can open doors to new understandings upon the verse seen above. In Ezekiel's verse, by taking the letter MEM

(מ) from the word MY PEOPLE (עמי) and then from right to left and from this letter, we count letters based on multiples of 4, the eighth letter (**4x2**) is the letter BET (ב) and from it, the fourth letter (**4x1**) is the letter DALET (ד), as follows:

לָכֵן הִנָּבֵא בֶן־אָדָם וְאָמַרְתָּ לְגוֹג כֹּה אָמַר אֲדֹנָי יְהוִֹה הֲלוֹא

בַּיּוֹם הַהוּא בְּשֶׁבֶת **עַמִּי** יִשְׂרָאֵל לְבֶ**טח תֵּ**דָע |

Ezekiel 38:14

Those are the initials of:

מ - משיח (Mashiach)

ב - בן (Ben)

ד - דוד (David)

Now we see why this is a prophecy related to Yeshua and why he was born of a virgin; it reveals that Yeshua, besides being Mashiach Ben Yosef, is also Mashiach Ben David, that is, two different facets, two different missions, of the same person. But is Yeshua the name of Ben David? Certainly, if we remember that the true name of Yeshua is actually Yehoshua, we have:

YEHOSHUA (יהושע)

י1 + ה5 + ו6 + ש3 + ע7

= 22 = **4**

Because Yeshua has no paternal seed, it makes him a tribe-free Jew, but at the same time, he is bound to different tribes according to his missions. By being Mashich Ben David, he is inevitably connected to the tribe of Judah and this is also revealed to us by Gematria:

HASHEVET YEHUDAH (השבט יהודה) - THE TRIBE OF JUDAH

ה5 + ש300 + ב2 + ט9 + י10 + ה5 + ו6 + ד4 + ה5

= 346 = 3+4+6 = 13 = **4**

The prophecy found in Isaiah 7, in addition to claiming that he would come from a virgin, also reveals that he is Mashiach Ben David and he is, therefore, connected to the tribe of Judah.

LEVI

אַל־תֹּאכְלוּ מִמֶּנּוּ נָא וּבָשֵׁל מְבֻשָּׁל בַּמָּיִם כִּי

אִם־צְלִי־אֵשׁ רֹאשׁוֹ עַל־כְּרָעָיו וְעַל־קִרְבּוֹ

Do not eat any of it raw, or cooked in any way with water,
but roasted over the fire — his head, legs, and entrails.

Exodus 12:9

Among all associations made and attributes that are related to Yeshua throughout the New Testament, the most complicated of them is when Yeshua is called priest, or high priest, for this may generate, as it actually does, many discord and motives for many to deal with a certain skepticism about the bible, for how can a messiah who should be king, be also a priest? One who is not even from the tribe of Levi?

Now of the things which we have spoken this is the sum:
We have such an high priest, who is set on the right
hand of the throne of the Majesty in the heavens.

Hebrews 8:1

However, with what has been seen so far, it is possible to begin to demystify this priestly association imposed on Yeshua. I cannot say whether the author of the book of Hebrews had a divine revelation or was aware of the subject matter dealt in this book, but the fact is, his claim about the connection between Mashiach and priesthood is totally plausible and coherent, since Yeshua, being a son of a virgin, may also be very well associate with the tribe of Levi, making him a great candidate to become a priest for Israel.

With a little of attention, we can find several facts that have occurred in Yeshua's life that link him to the priesthood as the above verse states, as for example his death that took place on a Pessach, which made him as the lamb that was sacrificed in this biblical feast, a sacrifice that could only be made by those from the tribe of Levi. Interestingly, coincidence or not, verse 9 from chapter 12 of Exodus is dealing precisely with the Pessach lamb and for this reason, it already begins to assemble some pieces of this puzzle.

If we separate the verse and leave only the part where it actually deals with the lamb, we have:

רֹאשׁוֹ עַל־כְּרָעָיו וְעַל־קִרְבּוֹ
his head, legs, and entrails

There are two pieces of very important information in these few extremely relevant words, the first is in its last word:

רֹאשׁוֹ עַל־כְּרָעָיו וְעַל־**קִרְבּוֹ**

The word translated as "entrails" is KIRBO (קרבו), this is a word formed by the root (ק-ר-ב), root which also forms the word KORBAN (קרבן), which means sacrifice (lamb).

The next day John sees Yeshua coming to him, and said, Behold
the Lamb of God, which takes away the sin of the world.
John 1:29

The second information is obtained only after we know the Gematria of the word Levi, the tribe of the priests of Israel:

LEVI (לוי)
10י + 6ו + 30ל
= 46 = 10 = **1**

Looking at this part of the verse, from left to right, from the FIRST (**1**) LAMED (ל), skipping **1** letter, we get the letter VAV (ו) and then the letter YUD (י) - thus forming the name LEVI (לוי) backwards.

רֹאשׁוֹ עַל־כְּרָעָ**י**ו **וְעַל**־קִרְבּוֹ

With this it is possible to establish a connection between the prophecy of the virgin, the tribe of Levi and the Pessach lamb seen in the verse above, but the question is: Does this connection extend to Yeshua as the high priest (and not to a simple priest) and to Yeshua the Mashiach Ben David?

LEVI (לוי)

ל3 + 6י + י1

= **10**

KORBAN (קרבן) - SACRIFICE (lamb)

ק1 + ר2 + ב2 + ן5

= **10**

KOHEN GADOL (כהן גדול) - HIGH PRIEST

כ2 + ה5 + ן5 + ג3 + ד4 + ו6 + ל3

= 28 = 2+8 = **10**

MASHIACH BEN DAVID (משיח בן דוד)

מ4 + ש3 + י10 + ח8 + ב2 + ן5 + ד4 + ו6 + ד4

= 46 = 4+6 = **10**

The only and true high priest who is bound to the tribe of Levi, the lamb of God, the one who will reign as Mashiach Ben David, is called YEHOSHUA, the one who came from Nazareth.

YEHOSHUA MENOTZERET (יהושע מנצרת) - YEHOSHUA FROM NAZARETH

י10 + ה5 + ו6 + ש3 + ע7 + מ4 + נ5 + צ9 + ר2 + ת4

= 55 = 5+5 = **10**

And this is confirmed once again in this little part taken from the verse of Exodus. Looking back to the verse and paying particular attention to the terms concerning the lamb, we have the following:

אִם־צְלִי־אֵשׁ רֹאשׁוֹ עַל־כְּרָעָיו וְעַל־קִרְבּוֹ

Do not eat any of it raw, or cooked in any way with water,
*but roasted over the fire — **his head, legs, and entrails.***

Exodus 12:9

רֹאשׁוֹ עַל־כְּרָעָיו וְעַל־קִרְבּוֹ
= **4**

The highlighted terms (which are the parts of the sacrificial animal) have a total value of 4, which is the same as Yeshua's real name:

YEHOSHUA (יהושע)
10י + 5ה + 6ו + 3שׁ + 7ע
= 31 = 3+1 = **4**

It's undeniable!

❖ ❖ ❖

EPHRATAH OF YEHUDAH

וְאַתָּה בֵּית־לֶחֶם אֶפְרָתָה צָעִיר לִהְיוֹת בְּאַלְפֵי יְהוּדָה מִמְּךָ לִי
יֵצֵא לִהְיוֹת מוֹשֵׁל בְּיִשְׂרָאֵל וּמוֹצָאֹתָיו מִקֶּדֶם מִימֵי עוֹלָם

And you, O Beit Lechem of Efratah, the smallest among the clans of Yehudah, from you will come forth to rule Israel for Me. One whose origin is of old, from ancient times.

Micah 5:1

And you Bethlehem, in the land of Judah, are not the least among the princes of Judah: for out of you shall come a Governor, that shall rule my people Israel.

Matthew 2:6 KJV

And you Beit Lechem of Yehudah, Ephratah, land of Yehudah, you are the smallest in the land of Yehudah, from you will come forth to me one to be the ruler in Israel.

Matthew 2:6

One of the prophecies that Matthew quotes in order to prove Yeshua's messianism is found in the book of Micah, where the prophet states that he who will reign over Israel shall come from Beit Lehem, a city in the region of Ephratah. However, if we compare the book of Micah with the Western translations of Matthew, it might give an impression that Matthew made a mistake, for he does not mention Ephratah as stated by the prophet, thus giving the impression of two different Beit Lechem. But what made me mention this slight error is, by mentioning that word (Ephratah), a word left aside by the KJV, makes all difference as we shall see next.

First of all, so that we may have an aid to understand it, let us look at a comment made by Rabbi Malbim about Micah's prophecy, the same one that Matthew quotes in his book:

> *And you, Beit Lechem, in order to awaken the*
> *ten scattered tribes of Israel, your king, Mashiach*
> *Ben Yosef, will be made brave for you, until the total*
> *restoration of Yehudah by Mashiach Ben David.*
>
> Rabbi Malbim, Micah 5:1

Malbim explains that this prophecy is not simply about Mashiach, but about a very specific mission of Mashiach, the mission of awakening the lost tribes of Israel. When Matthew associates this prophecy with Yeshua, he automatically declares that he is Mashiach Ben Yosef, and this is also confirmed by Yeshua himself when he mentions his real mission:

> *And Yeshua said to him, I was not sent except to*
> *the lost sheep of the House of Israel.*
>
> Matthew 15:24

But the question is, how can we prove that this prophecy of Micah really deals with Mashiach Ben Yosef and, what is the connection that Beit Lechem, the city where Yeshua was born, has with Mashiach Ben Yosef? In order that we may understand the message, we should not look at the prophecy of Micah, but rather at another passage found in the Tanakh that deals with the same terms, but from a different perspective:

> *These were the sons of Chur, the firstborn of Ephratah*
> *and the father of Beit Lechem.*
>
> I Chronicles 4:4b

This passage changes everything, Beit Lechem and Efratah are not just two locations, but also two people. According to the book of I Chronicles, Efratah was the father of Chur who was the father of Beit Lechem. It is precisely this passage that reveals to us what is happening in the book of Matthew and the connection he makes between Yeshua and Mashiach Ben Yosef. As prophecies are mystical revelations, we must analyze them mystically. The passage in I Chronicles reveals that Beit Lechem is the son of Chur, who is the first-born of Efratah. The prophet however, makes a direct connection between the grandson and the grandfather, which is a very common thing in the Tanakh, as if he called Beit Lechem the son of EF-RATAH, without mentioning Chur.

With all of this in mind, let's analyze these people using the Gematria and we shall see the message that it deliveries to us:

BEIT LECHEM BEN EFRATAH (בית לחם בן אפרתה)
- BEIT LECHEM SON OF EFRATAH
700ן + 2ב + 600ם + 8ח + 30ל + 400ת + 10י + 2ב
+ 1א + 80פ + 200ר + 400ת + 5ה
= 2438 = 2 + 4 + 3 + 8 = **17**

*Gematria with sofit

MASHIACH BEN YOSEF (משיח בן יוסף)
80ף + 60ס + 6ו + 10י + 50ן + 2ב + 8ח + 10י + 300ש + 40מ
= 566 = 5 + 6 + 6 = **17**

*Gematria without sofit

Both have the Gematria's value of 17, which, according to my point of view, confirms many things. Matthew is able to use this prophecy to show that Yeshua was Mashiach Ben Yosef, for he came from Beit Lechem, just as Rabbi Malbim teaches that Mashiach Ben Yosef would come from there. Matthew also confirms that his mission is exclusively for the house of Israel, as mentioned by Malbim in his commentary, as prophesied by Micah when he quotes that he came to Israel and again, by Yeshua himself, when he said:

And Yeshua said to him, I was not sent except to

the lost sheep of the House of Israel.

Matthew 15:24

This has a very deep and delicate thing. Many believe that Yeshua came to save the Gentiles, in fact, this is not his main mission. It is true that many Gentiles had access to the Bible and to the knowledge of the God of Israel through his death, but that was only a "blessing that overflowed the cup".

Because the descendants of the Kingdom of Israel, the lost tribes, were scattered throughout the world and assimilated by foreign cultures, they became "Gentiles" in a certain way. The mission of Mashiach Ben Yosef, in this case, Yeshua's, is precisely to bring these people back to the God of Israel and to the Torah. As they are among the Gentiles, it was the Gentiles that the work of Yeshua intended to reach, but with the real intention of reaching out these lost tribes. We do not know who the descendants of these tribes are, but as already discussed in this book, these people have a "spark" within themselves, a "spark" given to all members of the People of Israel in their earliest days. When the knowledge of the true Yeshua, the Torah, and the will of the One God are revealed to them, they will automatically feel something burning inside of them, which will lead them back to the Creator.

This will not happen to everyone who knows God or His Word or is part of a church, for simply knowing God doesn't make one His servant. These people, despite having been given this chance as a reflection of the search for the lost tribes, will never accept the God of Israel in the way that He wants to be accepted, that is, Torah for these people will be an absurd thing. This is why there is a roman jesus, for he serves this people who wants no connection with the true God and His Torah.

Many will never accept a Mashiach who is not in conformity with Christian theology, many will never accept a God other than the roman jesus, many will never accept the yoke of the Torah, even those inside temples, hearing and learning about the God of Israel and His Word. On the other hand, others under the same yoke, by hearing about these things, will have an awaken as never seen before and quickly, without knowing the motives and without someone having to convince them, will accept all these things and will have their lives immediately transformed. These are the descendants of the lost tribes of Israel and the targets of the work of Mashiach Ben Yosef.

The prophecy from Micah also reveals why Yeshua was not accepted by the Jews, for Jews, as we know them today and as they were in the first century, are not from the House of Israel, but rather from the House of Yehudah, and to the House of Yehudah, the Mashiach will be Mashiach Ben David, as Gematria reveals to us:

YEHUDAH (יהודה)

5ה + 4ד + 6ו + 5ה + 1י

21 = 2+1 = **3**

MASHIACH BEN DAVID (משיח בן דוד)

4ד + 6ו + 4ד + 700ן + 2ב + 8ח + 10י + 300ש + 40מ

1074 = 1+0+7+4 = 12 = 1+2 = **3**

From what we can see, for the House of Yehudah, for the Jews, the Mashiach will be at his coming as Mashiach Ben David, and for the House of Israel, because they are among the Gentiles, he will come (or came) as Mashiach Ben Yosef. His work will reach all the nations with the intention of lighting the "spark" within the descendants of the lost tribes; if anyone understands it, even if they are not descendants of these tribes, one can also be grafted unto the olive tree of Israel.

Certainly, both Mashiach Ben Yosef and Mashiach Ben David are the same, only two different missions. This is confirmed in another passage of the Tanakh:

> *David was the son of a certain Ephratite of Beit Lehem
> in Yehudah, named Yessi. He had eight children, and in
> Shaul's day, this man was old, advanced in age.*
> I Samuel 17:12

In a single passage we have a connection of Ephratah and Beit Lechem with King David. Ephratah and Beit Lechem now allude to king David and for this reason, to Mashiach Ben David himself, thus showing that both are intertwined, both are the same.

THE GIFTS

שִׁפְעַת גְּמַלִּים תְּכַסֵּךְ בִּכְרֵי מִדְיָן וְעֵיפָה כֻּלָּם מִשְּׁבָא
יָבֹאוּ זָהָב וּלְבוֹנָה יִשָּׂאוּ וּתְהִלֹּת יְהוָה יְבַשֵּׂרוּ

Dust clouds of camels shall cover you, Dromedaries of Midian and Ephah. They all shall come from Sheba; They shall bear gold and frankincense, And shall herald the glories of the LORD.

Isaiah 60:6

They went into the house, found him and his mother Miriam, knelt before him, honored him, opened their sacks and brought to him gifts of gold, frankincense and myrrh, that is, mira.

Matthew 2:11

One of the greatest mysteries of the gospels concerns this group of men known as the "wise men". Nothing is reported about their origins, their faith, how they knew about Yeshua and how they understood him; nothing besides the region from which they came from and how they reached their destination.

According to New Testament accounts, these men came from the region of Babylon, present-day Iran, a region where there was a strong development of astrology and strong mystique beliefs on the stars; many in that region based their decisions and routine on what the stars "revealed" to them, so much so that the gospel itself states that these "wise men" learned about the birth of Yeshua through the star movements.

There is much speculation about these figures; but according to my point of view, I believe they were men connected with the Zoroaster faith, who held a belief in one God and in which

Cyrus, king of Persia, called by God as "my servant", was part of. Zoroatrism had a strong influence on Judaism and many of its ideas can be seen in the words of Yeshua and for this reason, many of this belief still exists in Christianity now a days, such as the belief in dualism for example; the existence of an evil that opposes the good was born in this religion and was eventually absorbed by the Jewish faith while the people were captive in Babylon. On the other hand, these "wise men" could be descendants of Hebrews who were taken to Babylon during the first exile, because after the rebuilding of Jerusalem, many did not return to Israel.

Regardless of who they are; according to the biblical accounts about them, it is clear that they were people with deep knowledge of the Jewish faith, the Torah, and the God of Israel, and it is on these factors that this study should be based on. As reported by Matthew, these men brought three items, gold, incense and myrrh, items that are widely commented by our sages:

> *For a woman who has just given birth myrrh represents the burnt offering, incense represents the food offering, and gold was donated to the Ark of the Covenant as a form of ASHAM.*
> Talmud of Babylon, Tractate Temurah 23

The Gemarah teaches us something very interesting here, something that begins to reveal the mysteries of the gifts brought to Yeshua. It begins by stating that these gifts are for women who have just had children, which makes total sense in this case, and then associates each of these items with three types of Temple offerings, the burnt offering (Ex 19), the food offering. (Lv 2) and the offering of ASHAM (Lv 4). Each of these offerings had a very specific symbology. The burnt offering required a flawless, spotless lamb, the firstborn and the most perfect one.

The firstborn of every creature.

Colossians 1:15

The next day John sees Yeshua coming to him, and said, Behold the Lamb of God, which takes away the sin of the world.
John 1:29

The food offering had the flour that represents perfection, the absence of leaven represents sinlessness, and the salt represents the power to purify.

*Be you innocent for you Father is **perfect**.*
Matthew 5:48

*Who did no **sin**, neither was guile found in his mouth.*
I Peter 2:22

*How God anointed Yeshua of Nazareth with the Holy Ghost and with power: who went about doing good, and **healing** all that were oppressed of the devil; for God was with him.*
Acts 10:38

The ASHAM offering, represented by the gold, deals with an atonement for sins when they occur involuntarily, such as when a man does not know that a particular practice makes him a sinner and finds it out later, or that a certain attitude innocently caused him to break some commandment. In this case, the ASHAM's offer was required.

Who his own self bore our sins in his own body on the tree...
I Peter 2:24

With this we can see the prophetic character of these gifts, but the intriguing thing is that it does not stop here, for our sages go deeper into some spiritual characteristics of these three items:

Myrrh for the redemption of breaking the positive commandments, gold for the redemption of breaking the negative commandments and incense for committing idolatry.
Mishnah Shekalim 6

According to the Mishnah, each item is also associated with a type of sin. Myrrh represents the forgiveness of sins concerning the positive commandments, that is, when man fails to do what God tells him to do. Gold is for the forgiveness of breaking the negative commandments, which are those that God says no and yet man does them, and lastly, incense, which as already seen in this book, was THE SIN (singular) that Yeshua took away through his death.

This shows us the knowledge these men had of both the Torah and the rabbinical teachings. Somehow they were also revealed all the redeeming work of Mashiach, for the gifts they brought to him are prophetic representations of all that Yeshua would ever do; This makes the understanding of these "wise men" even more nebulous.

THE PROPHETIC HONOR

By Gematria, the sum of the letters found Isaiah's prophetic verse has a total value of 4247. Throughout the Tanakh, there are some verses that share that same total value. The one I am going to use is found in the book of Numbers, and it deals with a subject totally foreign to the subject we've been seeing so far, but this verse has a commentary with a impressive insight from one of the greatest Sephardic sages, Rabbi Abarbanel, descended from the line of king David, which I would like to point out.

וַיֹּאמֶר יְהֹוָה אֶל־מֹשֶׁה עֲלֵה אֶל־הַר הָעֲבָרִים הַזֶּה
וּרְאֵה אֶת־הָאָרֶץ אֲשֶׁר נָתַתִּי לִבְנֵי יִשְׂרָאֵל

The LORD said to Moses, Ascend these heights of Avarim and view the land that I have given to the Israelite people.

Numbers 27:12

Due to Moses' honor, Hashem told him to go up to the mountain and see the land and to make him realize that Joshua (Yehoshua) is ready to come. And from now on, may

> *the children of Israel treat Joshua (Yehoshua) with honor.*
> Abarbanel, Numbers 27:12

According to Rabbi Abarbanel, God commanded Moses to go up the mountain not only to see the land, but also to honor him and to show him that Joshua was ready to come. The name Joshua, Yehoshua in Hebrew, is not the original name of Joshua, but Hoshea, that name was changed by God, just as Yaakov's name was changed to Israel.

Rabbi Abarbanel talks about one named Yehoshua, which is Yeshua's real name, Yehoshua Ben Yosef. The interesting thing here is that Rabbi Abarbanel does not say that Yehoshua is ready to go, or to enter, into the land of Israel, but rather to come. From this comment we can understand some things that are not so clear in the Torah; What God may have shown Moses wasn't simply the land of Israel, but actually, God showed him the redeeming work of Mashiach. I believe that Moses not only knew this plan of God, but also, on the top of that mountain, he saw all the redemption of the people of Israel, he got to know his name and was revealed to him the honor that should be given to this Yehoshua by the house of Israel.

Perhaps, this is why this understanding about Moses and Mashiach is hidden in a prophecy that deals with the birth of Yeshua (Is 60:6), for what happened at that mountain with Moses, happened just before the land of Israel were born, and due to the creation of Israel, Mashiach was made ready by God to come to His people.

But how to prove it? Well, we just have to look at where God tells Moses to go, TO THE HEIGHTS OF AVARIM (אל הור העברים):

EL HOR HA'AVARIM (אל הור העברים) - TO
THE HEIGHTS OF AVARIM

$$4ם + 1' + 2ר + 2ב + 7ע + 5ה + 2ר + 6ו + 5ה + 3ל + 1א$$
$$= 38$$

YESHUA HAMASHIACH (ישוע המשיח)
$$8ח + 1' + 3ש + 4מ + 5ה\ 7ע + 6ו + 3ש + 1'$$
$$= 38$$

When Israel was created was the moment that God brought into this reality the redemption plan of Mashiach, and showed it to Moses; a plan that became real and palpable at the moment that those gifts were brought to Yeshua, this is why there was a prophecy about the gifts and why they were reported by the new testament's authors, for they reveal that this birth became real when Moses climbed that mountain. Nothing is by chance, not even the most simple and irrelevant things.

It is fantastic!

THE RAMAH'S CRY

כֹּה | אָמַר יְהוָֹה קוֹל בְּרָמָה נִשְׁמָע נְהִי בְּכִי תַמְרוּרִים רָחֵל מְבַכָּה עַל־בָּנֶיהָ מֵאֲנָה לְהִנָּחֵם עַל־בָּנֶיהָ כִּי אֵינֶנּוּ

Thus said Adonai: a voice is heard in Ramah, wailing, bitter weeping, Rachel weeping her children. She does not want to be comforted, for they are gone.

Jeremiah 31:15

Then was fulfilled what the prophet Yrmiahu said. A voice is heard in Ramah, lamentations and bitter weeping, Rachel weeping for her son and so on.

Matthew 2:17-18

Matthew quotes this prophecy shortly after the account of the massacre caused by Horodos, when, in search of Yeshua, he orders the slaughtering of all the male newborns. The fact that Jeremiah's prophecy deals with "weeping" and "death" of children, gives us a simple impression that Matthew mention was made because of the act of this murderer.

But if we look closely at the prophecy, it does not make much sense with that simple fact, for what does the matriarch Rachel have to do with that slaughter, since she was not even present at that moment?

Well, Rachel was the wife of Yaakov, the mother of Yosef and Benjamin. The Torah tells us that when Yaakov's favorite son, Yosef, was taken into captivity, his brothers told his father that he was killed and for years Yaakov wept for the loss of his son. Many years later, his brothers found him alive in Egypt and as the story develops, Benjamin, for being the youngest, ended up serving as a rescue tool to rid Yaakov's family from hunger and death.

If we make a simple connection with what has been seen until now, the two tribes from the sons of Yosef belonged to the Kingdom of Israel, they are two of the tribes lost in the world. In contrast, the tribe of Benjamin, as the tribe of Judah, were part of the Kingdom of South, the Kingdom of Yehudah, which was not dispersed and assimilated by the nations.

With this in mind, we can understand that just as one day Yaakov cried for having lost Yosef, Rachel's cry has the same symbology, the loss of her son Yosef to the nations of the world. But Benjamin, who represents the Kingdom of Yehudah, from which Mashiach Ben Yosef legally comes from, will serve as a ransom for Yosef and for his brothers, as we have seen so far. This idea is confirmed by the prophet Jeremiah himself in the following two verses:

> *Thus said Adonai, restrain your voice from weeping,*
> *your eyes from shedding the tears, for there is a reward*
> *for your labor, Adonai says, for they shall return from the*
> *lands of the enemy. And there will be hope at the end. Says*
> *Adonai, for your children will return to their country.*
> Jeremiah 31:16-17

Jeremiah, by continuing his prophecy, says that Adonai will return the sons of Rachel from the lands of the enemy, that is, those who have been assimilated by the nations will return to the land of Israel. Another interesting point to note is the word Ramah; there was a city in the territory of Benjamin called Ramah, which was right on the border with the tribe of Manasseh, one of the sons of Yosef. This city, after the separation of Israel in two kingdoms, ended up being annexed to the territory of the north, thus being part of the tribe of Manasseh. This is the city that made the connection between the two tribes that represented the two sons of Rachel, Manasseh of Yosef and Benjamin, and it is a city that ended up being lost along with the rest of the Kingdom of Israel.

The use of this prophecy by Matthew goes far beyond the atrocity caused by Horodos at that time, it shows that Mashiach Ben Yosef, who will come from the Kingdom of South, will bring back the lost son of Rachel, that is, he will serve as a rescue tool in order to save the lost tribes as Benjamin did.

EGYPT

כִּי נַעַר יִשְׂרָאֵל וָאֹהֲבֵהוּ וּמִמִּצְרַיִם קָרָאתִי לִבְנִי

I fell in love with Israel When he was still a child;
And I have called My son ever since Egypt.

Hosea 11:1

It came to pass when king Horodos died, the angel of Adonai
appeared in a dream to Yosef in Egypt. Saying, arise, take
the boy and his mother and go to the land of Israel, because
those who were seeking the boy to kill him are dead.

Matthew 2:19-20

Our sages' interpretation of this Hosea's verse makes no reference to Mashiach at all, for they say that this "son" that appears in this passage is Israel itself. With a look at other passages in the Tanakh, we shall see that God sees the people of Israel not actually as a son, but as something else, something even More deeper:

It will not be like the covenant I made with their
fathers, when I took them by the hand to lead them
out of the land of Egypt, a covenant which they broke,
though I espoused them, declares the LORD.

Jeremiah 31:32

Turn back, rebellious children, declares the LORD. Since
I have espoused you, I will take you, one from a town
and two from a clan, and bring you to Zion.

Jeremiah 3:14

According to God Himself, His bride, whom He has already espoused, is the people of Israel, something that contradicts the poor Christian theology, that claims that the church is the bride. Anyways, with that in mind, we cannot see the "son" in this passage as representing Israel, but rather Mashiach. For this reason I decided to make an analysis of this verse, because as I understand it, it is related to Mashiach and is a prophecy that is in agreement with a fact that occurred in the life of Yeshua as described in the book of Matthew.

The first thing we need to take into account in this prophecy is God's statement about his love for Israel, in this case, the Kingdom of Israel and not the people in general, for in verse 2 the prophet begins to list sins that were practiced by the people who were part of this kingdom and not sins committed by Israel as a whole, such as worshiping the god Baal for example and the mentioning the tribe of Ephraim, which belonged to the northern kingdom. From this, it is clear Yeshua's directly connection with the Kingdom of Israel, for from this verse we can understand that Yeshua was called by the love God has for the descendants of these lost tribes.

Going back to the words of the prophet Hosea, the verse states that God called his son from Egypt, the one who is called is the one who hears the call, the one who gives ears. This is interesting, for there is a parashah called HAAZINU (Deut 32:1 - Deut 32:52), which means "to give ear", "to listen to", and even more interesting is that the first verse of this parashah (Deuteronomy 32:1) has a total numerical value of 2145 and this is the same total numerical value from the above prophecy, Hosea 11:1. This leads me to believe that the answers we need lie in the message behind this parashah.

PARASHAT HAAZINU (Dt 32:1-52)
An interesting thing we have in the New Testament is the discrepancy concerning some topics, such as the strong ap-

proach to grace, something that does not occur so widely in the Tanakh. The question is, how can the New Testament's grace and the seemingly merciless judgment of the Tanakh be able to establish a balance in the spiritual reality that we live in today? I mean, how can we see God's grace from the Tanakh and how can we see God's judgement from the New Testament, a judgment that actually is not so merciless as many think, in our lives? To understand this, we need only to look at this prophecy, the prophecy about the calling of Yeshua back from Egypt, and see it not as a simple fact that took place in his life, but rather as a prophecy about a spiritual deed from God; for at the moment of this calling, something happened, something that most people are not able to see, for it was at this very moment that a balance between grace and judgment were given and revealed to those who are able to understand them.

HAAZINU, one of Torah's last parashot, comes in the form of a song made by Moses shortly before his death. This song, Haazinu, praises the Creator and the power of bestowal. It points out that we must always remember to see God's hands in all that happens in this earth, the value of loving the others, which is the greatest teaching of the Torah, and how is the right way to do everything we need to do. "Love your neighbor as yourself" is more than just a maxim, it is the purpose of each and every action, a rule that includes all our efforts.

The song praises the people of Israel - those desires in us that want to rise, to be like the Creator, something that creates a goal of bestowal. The song praises all these desires, desires called as "the people of Israel" for they are the greatest and most important desires a man can achieve This parashah has 52 verses, a number that corresponds to this earthly reality, as well as twice the value of God's name that is above all names, the tetragram (26 = יהוה). This shows us that the physical world is a reflection of the higher worlds, just as everything we see in our reality is the result of what is within us.

HAAZINU, in a literal translation means "to give ears" or "to listen to". But what does it really mean to "listen" to something? What is the deep meaning of these words of Moses? Listening to something is not just about hearing, but about balancing, that is, man hears something and if he listens to that something, then that something gets into his heart and into his mind and he is able to create a balance with this new information that transforms both his reason and his emotions. The root of the word HAAZINU (האזינו) is ALEF (א), ZAIN (ז) and NUN (נ), this is the same root as the word EAR (אוזן) - ozen - and the word BALANCE (אזן) - izen.

Everything that balances man's life comes by hearing, this is why Deuteronomy 6:4 begins with LISTEN, and it is also why faith comes by LISTENING, for the real listening is not simply listening or hearing, but rather it is the pursue of a balance between the emotional side and the rational side within our beings. To make this clearer, we only have to understand the labyrinthitis, a disease that, when affects man, causes him to completely lose his balance and makes him unable to move, and such disorder is caused in the labyrinths within the human ear.

The Zohar teaches that all fruits are connected with Malchut's sefirah, the sefirah that represents the human, physical and finite reality; all fruits except the apple, because, according to the Zohar, this fruit represents the balance between three higher sefirot, that are GVURAH (judgment), CHESSED (grace) and TIFERET (compassion). The balance between these three manifestations of God, judgment, grace and compassion is what strengthens man and makes him to truly recognize the Creator. Judgment without grace there would be no mercy, grace without judgment there would be no justice and judgment without compassion there would be no kindness, that is, to recognize these attributes of God a balance is mandatory, we need to "give ears", we need the IZEN that comes from OZEN according to HAAZINU.

Interesting, because one of the works of Mashiach Ben Yosef is the teaching of the Torah. When man understands its true mysteries, he begins to seek God in a different way, a way where he no longer have to be punished for disobedience, for it will be a way much closer to a good judgment from God, as well as to His grace and compassion. This leads me to understand that the prophecy about the calling back from Egypt tells us that Yeshua would come with such a Torah teaching, a teaching that would reveal the true relationship that the people should have with God, how they should observe the Torah, and how they should seek the Creator in the proper way. Ben Yosef's teaching brings a balance, a balance that cannot be reached by religions, both Judaism and Christianity, a balance that is not bound by human theology and religious dogma; It is a balance between the physical and the spiritual world, because, as seen above, HAAZINU also teaches that everything that happens here is a reflection of what is decided in the heavens. With the Torah of Mashiach it is possible to change these predeterminations, to change the so called "destiny", in order to seek a closer relationship with God and to have a greater balance about what we receive from God.

This is my understanding of the prophecy about the calling from Egypt.

But there is more about it.

LIBRA
Parashat HAAZINU has another very interesting facet. Its root is also the root of the word MOZNAYIM (מאזנים) which is the Hebrew name of the libra sign, and the most interesting thing is that this parashah is read in the month of Tishrei, precisely in the month governed by this sign. Maybe that might give us some more information about the prophecy found in

Hosea.

At that time, after those days, the sun will darken, the moon
will not give forth its light, the stars will fall from the heavens
and all hosts (chail) of the heavens will tremble. And then the
sign of the son of man will appear in heaven and all the families
of the earth will weep and will see the son of man among the
clouds of heaven with a great host (chail) and with a dreadful
appearance. And he will send his angels with a trumpet and
with a loud voice to gather all his chosen ones from the four
winds of the heavens, from one end of heaven unto the other.

Matthew 24:29-31

כִּי־כוֹכְבֵי הַשָּׁמַיִם וּ**כְסִי־לֵ**יהֶם לֹא יָהֵלּוּ אוֹרָם חָשַׁךְ
הַשֶּׁמֶשׁ בְּצֵאתוֹ וְיָרֵחַ לֹא־יַגִּיהַ אוֹרוֹ

The stars and constellations of heaven Shall not
give off their light; The sun shall be dark when it
rises, And the moon shall diffuse no glow.

Isaiah 13:10

Yeshua quotes the verse of Isaiah almost in its entirety, except for a term added by him, translated as hosts in verses
29 and 30 (see above). The word CHAIL (חיל) has some mean-
ings, such as "force", "hosts", "force that holds something together", but its Aramaic meaning is the collective noun for
stars which, in other words, means constellation. This leads
to the understanding that, like Isaiah, Yeshua is also speaking
about something hidden.

In Isaiah's verse, the word translated as "constellations", in
Hebrew, is KSILIM (כסילים), plural of KSIL (כסיל).

KSIL does not mean "constellation", but it is rather the name
of a specific star located in the South Pole. This star is known
as "the sign that camels will die" as it only becomes visible
in the northern hemisphere in midsummer when the camels
are exposed to extreme temperatures and die from the heat.

These hidden terms can only be understood through the mystique and astrological knowledge of the ancient sages.

Ksil is the Star in the heart of the constellation Scorpio, southern equinoctial point. For a long time the constellation Libra was considered to be part of the constellation Scorpio, the former being the center of the latter. According to the great Kabbalist Rabbi Ibn Ezra, Ksil was the heart star of Scorpio, representing the center of this constellation, but now a distinction has been made, making this star part of the Libra constellation.

LIBRA (TISHREI) - The period of Libra is the most delicate one, for it is the season that holds two important appointed times, Rosh Hashanah (new year) and ten days later, Yom Kippur (day of forgiveness). Our sages teach that these ten days between the feasts are precisely the time when the heavens will be open so that we can reflect on our sins and truly seek forgiveness for them; then, when the day of Yom Kippur comes, God will give His sentence on us. For this reason the symbol for this time of the year is the scale.

Yom Kippur is the most important appointed time of the Torah, it is an ordinance represented by the sacrifices that were brought to the Temple. The star of Ksil has a symbology associated with Yom Kippur, as it is part of the constellation that is represented by a scale, thus making a reference to God's judgment day.

The word Ksil appears elsewhere in the Torah, but this time not as a star or a constellation, but in reference to the korban itself, the sacrifice:

וְאֵת שְׁתֵּי הַכְּלָיֹת וְאֶת־הַחֵלֶב אֲשֶׁר עֲלֵהֶן אֲשֶׁר עַל־הַ**כְּסָלִים**
וְאֶת־הַיֹּתֶרֶת עַל־הַכָּבֵד עַל־הַכְּלָיֹות יְסִירֶנָּה

He shall then present from the sacrifice of well-being,
as an offering by fire to the LORD, the fat that covers the
entrails and all the fat that is about the entrails.

Leviticus 3:4

In this passage we have the word Ksil in association with the sacrifice to be brought to the Temple. Remembering that those rules found on these Torah verse were to be observed in both Passover and Yom Kippur. And for this reason I believe that this is a prophecy concerning Mashiach Ben David, for it might reveal the time of year he will come, as seen above, in the ten days between Rosh Hashanah and Yom Kippur, this is why Yeshua probably mentioned it.

So may it be in our days.

THE STRANGER

A second Torah passage that has the same numerical value as Hosea's prophecy has, the value of 2145, speaks about a theme much addressed by Paul in his letters:

לֹא תַטֶּה מִשְׁפַּט **גֵּר** יָתוֹם וְלֹא תַחֲבֹל בֶּגֶד אַלְמָנֶה

*You shall not subvert the rights of the **stranger** or the fatherless; you shall not take a widow's garment in pawn.*

Deuteronomy 24:17

The death of Yeshua, something that brought the Torah to all nations in order to gather the Kingdom of Israel's descendants, certainly also opened the doors for the stranger who wishes to be part of that people. It is like the blessing that overflows from the cup, for when the person who does not possess the spark of the tribes of Israel, understands, knows, and submits himself to the will of God and His Torah, he will also receive that spark and automatically be grafted into that olive tree, into this people:

For if you were cut out of the olive tree which is wild by nature, and were grafted contrary to nature into a good olive tree: how much more shall these, which be the natural branches, be grafted into their own olive tree?

Romans 11:24

This teaches us that the calling of Yeshua from Egypt is not a mere story in which he goes from one place to another, but it is the revelation of why he was called. He is raised by God as Mashiach Ben Yosef, who would teach the Torah and die so that these teachings would reach the nations of the world in search of the lost sheep of Israel who were absorbed by them, as well as to give a chance to those who did not come from the 12 tribes to hear about and to know who the true God is, and thus they may be adopted into His people. That is the real reason why Yeshua had to go to Egypt in order to be "called" and this prophecy was related.

CONFIRMATION ON THE KINGDOM OF ISRAEL
The third verse that has the numerical value of 2145 is found in the book of Nehemiah:

בְּנֵי בֵצָי שְׁלֹשׁ מֵאוֹת עֶשְׂרִים וְאַרְבָּעָה
The sons of Bezai—324.

Nehemiah 7:23

This passage may be the confirmation that the prophecy deals with the Kingdom of Israel. To make it clear, we must divide this verse into two parts, the first is the term BNEI BET-ZAI (בני בצי) - *the sons of Bezai* - and the second is the number 324. BNEI BETZAI (בני בצי) has the following numeric value:

BNEI BETZAI (בני בצי) - SONS OF BEZAI
ב2 + 5נ + 1י + 2ב + 9צ + 1י
20 = **2**

The number 2 is the number representing the KINGDOM OF ISRAEL (מלכות ישראל):

MALCHUT ISRAEL (מלכות ישראל) - KINGDOM OF ISRAEL
מ4 + 3ל + 2כ + 6ו + 4ת + 1י + שׁ4 + 2ר + 1א + 3ל
29 = 2+9 = 11 = 1+1 = **2**

The second part, the number 324, is written in full as seen in the verse (שְׁלֹשׁ מֵאוֹת עֶשְׂרִים וְאַרְבָּעָה), and the total value of those letters is 1981; this is the same value of a passage that is found in the book of Leviticus:

> *Do not turn to idols or make molten gods for yourselves:*
> *I the LORD am your God.*
>
> Leviticus 19:4

Now it gets interesting, because if we look at why the Kingdom of Israel was destroyed, we will see that it was precisely because of what God just warned in the passage above, idolatry.

> *Jeroboam fortified Shechem in the hill country of Ephraim*
> *and resided there; he moved out from there and fortified Peniel.*
> *Jeroboam said to himself, "Now the kingdom may well return to*
> *the House of David. If these people still go up to offer sacrifices*
> *at the House of the LORD in Jerusalem, the heart of these people*
> *will turn back to their master, King Rehoboam of Judah; they*
> *will kill me and go back to King Rehoboam of Judah". So the king*
> *took counsel and made two golden calves. He said to the people,*
> *"You have been going up to Jerusalem long enough. This is your*
> *god, O Israel, who brought you up from the land of Egypt!"*
>
> I Kings 12:25-28

By this we understand that the passage of Nehemiah, occultly confirms that the Kingdom of Israel was destroyed due to their idolatry and it also confirms the connection between this passage with the prophetic passage from Hosea about Yeshua's call, for it leads us to the understanding that he was called to the lost sheep from that kingdom, so the descendants of these tribes may listen (HAAZINU) to his words so they may be able to return to the Torah, thus leaving the idolatry behind.

Through this passage from Nehemiah, we see that Yeshua is

"called" to gather the descendants of this people and to open the doors to the strangers, so all may have the opportunity to listen to God and to get rid of idolatrous religions and creeds.

For thus said the LORD: Cry out in joy for Jacob, Shout at the crossroads of the nations! Sing aloud in praise, and say: Save, O LORD, Your people, The remnant of Israel. I will bring them in from the northland, Gather them from the ends of the earth. The blind and the lame among them, Those with child and those in labor. In a vast throng they shall return here.
Jeremiah 31: 7-8

TZITZIT

וְזָרְחָה לָכֶם יִרְאֵי שְׁמִי שֶׁמֶשׁ צְדָקָה וּמַרְפֵּא בִּכְנָפֶיהָ
וִיצָאתֶם וּפִשְׁתֶּם כְּעֶגְלֵי מַרְבֵּק

But for you who fear My name a sun of victory
shall rise to bring healing under his wings. You shall
go forth and stamp like stall-fed calves.

Malachi 3:20

And, behold, a woman with a flow of blood for twelve years,
came up behind him and touched the Tzitzit of his Talit.
She said in her heart: If I touch his talit, I will be healed
immediately. He turned his face and said to her: Be strong
*my daughter, the **fear** for Adonai, blessed be He (Baruch*
hu) healed you. At that very hour she was healed.

Matthew 9:20-22

The New Testament, although many people do not understand, makes it very clear how Torah's observant Yeshua was. For this reason, there is no doubt that he wore his tzitzit all the time, just as the Torah commands it.

According to the Torah itself, the garments were created and given to man because of Adam's sin which, by having consumed the fruit of the Tree of the Knowledge of Good and Evil, became aware of the evil inclination within him, thus realizing that certain parts of his body were associated with physical pleasures. For this reason, the Creator decided to make clothes for him and such a concept of "getting dressed" never left human reality. I believe it is for this reason that the Torah orders that tzitzit should be attached to one's garments, for it serves two purposes: as a reminder for us to stand guard against our evil inclination and to overcome it through the commandments. The garments are nothing more than a memorial of the price to be paid if we do not pay attention to what God wants from us, as happened with Adam.

The tzitzit is part of the daily dress of the People of Israel, it has always been attached in the daily garments to constantly remember the commandments of the One God. This commandment has a unique symbolism and generates an exclusive approach to God. An interesting thing about the tzitzit is that one of them is cut off from a dying person's garment, as it represents the end of his obligations to the Torah. That is why in 1 Samuel 24, David cuts the "edges" of King Shaul's garments; in fact, he cuts his tzitzit, representing the death of his reign.

The tzitzit is a fringe attached in the garments, but it is not part of them. There are 5 intertwined cotton threads with 8 knots, giving a total of 13 different stitches. If we use Gematria and calculate the numerical value of the word tzitzit in Hebrew, we get the value of 600 and adding both (its numerical value plus the number of stitches), we get the value of 613. 613 is precisely the number of commandments found in the Torah, 613 mitzvot. That is why God commands the use of the tzitzit as a reminder of His commandments, all 613. It should be affixed to the four corners of the garment or of the Tallit (prayer robe).

In first-century Israel, it was customary for men to wear a simple tunic called haluk, both at home and on the go. When in public places, it was customary to wear over the haluk another quadrangular robe called Tallit, which was all the way down from the shoulders to the feet and served as climate protection. At each of the four corners of the Tallit, the Tzitzit were attached in obedience to this biblical commandment.

There is a power and an immeasurable spiritual secret behind this commandment, so strong that Rabbi Shimon Bar Yochai says that the one who uses the tzitzit during his prayers receives the Shekhinah over him. Such power, which many do not understand, was well known by this woman with the blood flow problem. If we look at the Torah, we can see where she got that faith from. In the Malachi passage above, the Hebrew word for "wings" (in some translations "borders") is "knafeiah", such a term appears throughout the Tanakh seventy-six times, and by adding seven to six, we shall have the number 13, which represents the five threads and the eight knots of the tzitzit.

וְזָרְחָה לָכֶם יִרְאֵי שְׁמִי שֶׁמֶשׁ צְדָקָה וּמַרְפֵּא בִּ**כְנָפֶיהָ**
וִיצָאתֶם וּפִשְׁתֶּם כְּעֶגְלֵי מַרְבֵּק

*But for you who fear My name a sun of victory shall
rise to bring healing under his wings (Knafeiah). You
shall go forth and stamp like stall-fed calves.*

Malachi 3:20

The prophet states that Mashiach will come bringing healing under his wings, under his knafeiah, which is nothing else but his own tzitzit itself. Malachi states that only those who fear Adonai's name (the tetragrammaton) will receive healing. When Yeshua realizes what is happening, he turns to the woman and says that her fear for Adonai (referring to the tetragram) had healed her, thus confirming what the prophet had said. With this understanding in mind, a passage in psalms becomes much clearer and more coherent:

בְּאֶבְרָתוֹ | יָסֶךְ לָךְ וְתַחַת־**כְּנָפָיו** תֶּחְסֶה צִנָּה וְסֹחֵרָה אֲמִתּוֹ
*He will cover you with His pinions; you will find refuge
under His wings (Knafeiah).*

Psalms 91:4

The healing came through a commandment of the Torah, through a belief in the Living Word of the Living God, a prophecy, the wings of Mashiach and the obedience that Yeshua had.

THE BROKEN MASHIACH

הֵן עַבְדִּי אֶתְמׇךְ־בּוֹ בְּחִירִי רׇצְתָה נַפְשִׁי נָתַתִּי רוּחִי עָלָיו מִשְׁפָּט לַגּוֹיִם יוֹצִיא
לֹא יִצְעַק וְלֹא יִשָּׂא וְלֹא־יַשְׁמִיעַ בַּחוּץ קוֹלוֹ
קָנֶה רָצוּץ לֹא יִשְׁבּוֹר וּפִשְׁתָּה כֵהָה לֹא יְכַבֶּנָּה לֶאֱמֶת יוֹצִיא מִשְׁפָּט
לֹא יִכְהֶה וְלֹא יָרוּץ עַד־יָשִׂים בָּאָרֶץ מִשְׁפָּט וּלְתוֹרָתוֹ אִיִּים יְיַחֵילוּ

This is My servant, whom I uphold, My chosen one, in whom I delight. I have put My spirit upon him, He shall teach the true way to the nations. He shall not cry out or shout aloud, Or make his voice heard in the streets. He shall not break even a bruised reed, Or snuff out even a dim wick. He shall bring forth the true way. He shall not grow dim or be broken Till he has established the true way on earth; And the coastlands shall await his teaching.

Isaiah 42:1-4

In order to fulfill what was spoken by Isaiah, Behold my servant whom I have selected, my chosen one with whom my soul is pleased, I will put my spirit upon him, and he will declare justice to the nations. He will not fear nor will he run nor shall one hear him in the street. A crushed reed he will not break and a dim wick he will not quench until he establishes justice forever. And in his name, the gentile hope.

Matthew 12:17-21

The mention of this prophecy by the author of the book of Matthew has already caused much debate and discord between Jews and Christians. The Jews claim that this quote is a huge mistake in the book of Matthew, because this prophecy was not fulfilled by jesus, since, according to the prophecy, God's chosen servant could not be injured without first establishing peace. As we know, this was not the case, as the world is not and has never been at peace. The Jews' argument about this prophecy makes perfect sense, jesus would not be the Mashiach.

On the Christian side, they claim that Jesus did establish peace, but not a world peace as the Jews had hoped for. The peace the christians claim to have been established is not quite "peace" in its literal sense, but the unification of the Gentiles with the Jews into one people, for all became as sons of God through their jesus.

According to my point of view, none of the explanations above are satisfactory. On the Jewish side, they are right, jesus did not fulfill this prophecy, just as any prophecy that concerns Mashiach, for he is not and never will be Mashiach. However, this jewish interpretation is not accurate, because it does not address Yeshua, but rather the mythical figure created by the fathers of the church. On the other hand, Christians think that Gentiles and Jews will all be the same, or better than them, but the reality is not quite that, Christians who will have to be more like the Jews and not the Jews more like Christians, it may seem to be the same thing, but it's not. Not that Judaism is a religion to be followed, but the Torah that represents them is what allows Jews a closer connection with the Creator, something that the gentiles need to understand. Another point to consider is that Yeshua did not come to any and all Gentiles, but to a very specific group that is scattered among the Gentiles, which is not known to anyone. Obviously, all those who, even without being part of this group, can and will be accepted into the People of Israel due to his teachings and sacrifice.

In order to understand what this prophecy talks about and why the author of the book of Matthew quotes it, we must ask two questions. First, does this prophecy really speak about Mashiach? Second, if so, which Mashiach?

To answer the first one, let's look at what some sages say in the Talmud:

> *He who sees a reed in a dream should rise early and recite: "A crushed reed he will not break" (Is 42:3), in honor to Mashiach.*
> Talmud of Babylon, Tractate Brakhot 56b

> *Rabbi Hiyya said to him: No, this refers to another verse, the one that speaks about Mashiach in Isaiah 42:3.*
> Talmud of Babylon, Tractate Yevamot 93b

The sages answer the first question and confirm what many deny, these verses speak about Mashiach and not about any prophet or anything. Now, in order to understand exactly what the prophet Isaiah refers to in his words, we must look at these verses in a slightly more mystical way.

In the first verse, in its original language, we have the following:

הֵן עַבְדִּי אֶתְמָךְ בּוֹ בְּחִירִי רָצְתָה נַפְשִׁי נָתַתִּי רוּחִי עָלָיו מִשְׁפָּט לַגּוֹיִם יוֹצִיא
This is My servant, whom I uphold, My chosen one,
in whom I delight. I have put My spirit upon him,
He shall teach the true way to the nations.

Isaiah 42:1

If we take the first three words that appear in this verse and look for their numerical value, we shall have:

HEN AVDI ETMAKH (הן עבדי אתמך)
5ה + 5ן + 7ע + 2ב + 4ד + 1י + 1א + 4ת + 4מ + 2ך
= **8**

Interesting, because this absolute value is the same as the absolute value of the name MASHIACH BEN YOSEF, as shown below:

MASHIACH BEN YOSEF (משיח בן יוסף)

4מ + 3ש + 1י + 8ח + 2ב + 5ן + 1י + 6ו + 6ס + 8ף

= **8**

This tells us that this verse deals with Mashiach Ben Yosef; not only the first verse, but the second one as well, for as we analyze the third verse using Gematria, just as the previous verse, we shall see that Isaiah's prophecy changes its object:

קָנֶה רָצוּץ לֹא יִשְׁבּוֹר וּפִשְׁתֶּה כֵהָה לֹא יְכַבֶּנָּה לֶאֱמֶת יוֹצִיא מִשְׁפָּט

He shall not break even a bruised reed, Or snuff out even
a dim wick. He shall bring forth the true way.

Isaiah 42:3

(קנה רצוץ לא ישבור)

1ק + 1נ + 5ה + 2ר + 9צ + 6ו + 9ץ + 3ל + 1א + 1י + 3ש + 2ב + 6ו + 2ר

= **10**

MASHIACH BEN DAVID (משיח בן דוד)

4מ + 3ש + 1י + 8ח + 2ב + 5ן + 4ד + 6ו + 4ד

= **10**

From verse three, Isaiah no longer deals with Mashiach Ben Yosef, but rather with Mashiach Ben David. As the author of the book of Matthew quotes only the first four verses of Isaiah 42, we understand that the first two deal with Mashiach Ben Yosef and the third and fourth with Mashiach Ben David. Perhaps this is why there are, in the midst of this mystical prophecy, some things that Yeshua has not accomplished yet, for it also speak about the second part of his mission, the one that has not taken place yet.

In order to clarify all of this, let's go through some rabbinic and Midrashim commentaries:

Mashiach Ben Yosef (Isaiah 42 - v1 and v2)

We should not be ashamed of the generation of Mashiach.
The Holy One, Blessed Be He, said to them: "This is My
servant, My chosen one, the one who pleases my soul, and
so forth" (Isaiah 42:1). At that moment, the Holy One,
Blessed Be He, will tell him: "Ephraim, Mashiach, My
Tzadik, I conceived you before the six days of creation.
Now my sorrow is for what thou shalt go through...

Midrash Psikta Rabbati 36:1

This Midrash reports some rather mystical things. First, it is directly related to the passage we are analyzing, as he himself mentions, Isaiah 42:1. Then he quotes both the word "Mashiach" and the name "Ephraim".

Ephraim was the firstborn of Yosef and it is by this name that many Midrashim refer to Mashiach Ben Yosef. Ephraim became a second term in reference to this facet of Mashiach, so we understand that this verse speaks precisely about Mashiach Ben Yosef. One other thing to note is, when the author speaks about the sorrow that God will have, it is in reference to Mashiach's death. So, it means that Ben Yosef had to die.

"He will teach the true way to the nations" (Isa 42:1), this
is the Torah that everyone will want to hear, his Torah.

Rashi, Isaiah 42:1

As we have already seen, two of the main missions of Mashiach Ben Yosef is to bring the Torah into the Gentile world and to teach how it is to be lived. Through Rabbi Rashi, we have another confirmation that this verse deals specifically with Mashiach Ben Yosef.

Now it is clear, as we read the first two verses again, we see that the servant chosen by Adonai is clearly Mashiach, but in this case, Mashiach Ben Yosef, for it was his mission to teach the nations the true ways and to reveal the Torah to the gentiles. If we look at Yeshua and see him as Mashiach Ben Yosef, the second verse makes perfect sense, for as much as he preached and taught, in the end, he was not heard by the Jews and was not understood by the Christians.

Mashiach Ben David (Isaiah 42 - v3 and v4)

"He shall not break" with the term ירוץ. *The form of this verb refers us to* ירון *as it appears in Prov. 29:6 and the meaning of this "joy" is that he will not die nor be overcome by the violence of men.*

Ibn Ezra, Isaiah 42:4

In this fantastic commentary, Rabbi Ibn Ezra takes the word YARUTZ (ירוץ) - *broken* - and compares its form with another word, YARUN (ירון) - *sing out* - in the way it appears in the book of Proverbs, thus making an analogy about this facet of Mashiach.

לֹא יִכְהֶה וְלֹא **יָרוּץ** עַד־יָשִׂים בָּאָרֶץ מִשְׁפָּט וּלְתוֹרָתוֹ אִיִּים יְיַחֵילוּ
*He shall not grow dim or be **broken** Till he has established the true way on earth; And the coastlands shall await his teaching.*

Isaiah 42:4

בְּפֶשַׁע אִישׁ רָע מוֹקֵשׁ וְצַדִּיק **יָרוּן** וְשָׂמֵחַ
*An evil man's offenses are a trap for himself, But the righteous **sing out** joyously.*

Proverbs 29:6

Ibn Ezra confirms Mashiach Ben David through the obvious, for this is not the facet of Mashiach that will suffer, but it will be the one who will sing out joyously as we see in the Proverb above, for he will not die and will not be overcome by the violence of men (Gog and Magog war that will precede Mashiach Ben David; he will not be defeated by it).

He will not be grow dim, for he will be the true Mashiach. The Laws of God and the leadership of Mashiach will be imposed even on the most distant islands of the world, and the Torah and worship of the true God will be spread to every corner.

Malbim, Isaiah 42:4

Also according to Malbim, in his commentary on verse four, he confirms that this verse deals precisely with the Age of Mashiach, which will be governed by Mashiach Ben David.

However, among all seen above, I believe that the author of the book of Matthew had one more reason to quote this prophecy and this reason is explained at the very beginning of the words of the prophet:

This is My servant…. (not servantS).

Adonai does not speak about two servants; even though the prophecy speaks of Mashiach Ben Yosef and Mashiach Ben David; he is called The Unique Servant, thus showing that both Ben Yosef and Ben David are one and the same, with only different facets, missions, and periods in history.

The purpose of this study is not to explain the prophecy itself, but to understand why the author of the book of Matthew linked it with Yeshua, for he wanted to prove that both Mashiach Ben Yosef, as well as Mashiach Ben David, are the same and he is Yeshua.

KNOWLEDGE
OF OLD

אֶפְתְּחָה בְמָשָׁל פִּי אַבִּיעָה חִידֹות מִנִּי־קֶדֶם

*I will open my mouth with parables, I will
preach with knowledge of old.*

Psalms 78:2

*All of those allegories Yeshua spoke to the crowds
and without an allegory he did not speak to them. To
fulfill what was said by the prophet, I will open my
mouth in allegories, I will utter riddles of old.*

Matthew 13:34-35

The teaching using parables is the oldest and most common method presented by the rabbis to teach the Torah's mysteries. In many parts of the Talmud and Gemarah, rabbis present their teachings in this way. One of the greatest rabbis in history, Rabbi Akiva, was one of the Talmud's greatest storytellers, his parables are widely known and bear great Torah revelations and moral teachings.

Yeshua, a rabbi from Rabbi Hillel's school, has brought many parables that, while revealing Torah secrets, go hand in hand with the moral teachings and thoughts of his master's school, which are reported in various passages in the Mishnah.

The great sage Alshich teaches that the parable method was developed so that the pagan people around the world would not misappropriate holy teachings. This is very clear when we look at Yeshua for example, who had his stories interpreted by Christian theology without the necessary background and knowledge, and so what we see today is a great Christian puritanism being preached and taught in place of what it should have be preached and taught.

But the subject of this study is not parables themselves, but the prophecy in question. This verse of Psalms is closely associated with Yeshua, for he is the greatest source of parables within the Christian milieu, but such a prophecy might well fit any rabbi, for this method is a commonplace among them all.

If we look at this Psalm in a messianic way, as the author of the book of Matthew suggests, it is possible to find many things about Mashiach Ben Yosef and his relationship with the Torah. According to our sages, the Torah should be taught in parables, the mysteries of the Torah should never be openly exposed, the same sages also teach that Mashiach Ben Yosef has the mission to teach the Torah by using parables and to show how it should be lived, as we can find throughout many commentaries:

> *IN PARABLES - it represents the teachings of the Torah.*
> Rashi, Psalm 78:2

> *The Almighty has made a covenant with Israel and by the Torah,*
> *Israel will not forget it, and by the Torah He will establish a*
> *testimony of Yaakov in Israel. Let no one say that the Psalms are*
> *not the Torah itself, for the Psalms mystify the Torah, for the*
> *Psalms make the Torah like parables. King Shlomo (Solomon)*
> *recommends that you understand the words of the sages and*
> *their riddles through the parables, as we see in his Proverbs.*
> Midrash Tehillim 78

> *The one who will go from place to place and will teach*
> *his parables from place to place and will take his*
> *Torah from place to place, is King Mashiach.*

Ruth Rabbah 8

From this we can see that the parable is the Torah itself and that Mashiach, who will come to teach the Torah, will teach it in parables. Therefore, what Yeshua has done is in full agreement with Mashiach Ben Yosef's facet.

> *The one who explains what is hidden - this was said*
> *about Yosef, and this is one of the missions of Mashiach*
> *Ben Yosef, his parables will be known to all generations.*
> *God's Torah will be known by the walk of Mashiach*
>
> Kol HaTor 2:122

OF OLD

There is much wisdom in the Tanakh that is not presented clearly. In this verse of Psalms there is a small word that can demystify many things about what has been said so far. The Word קדם that appears in this verse, is also similarly presented elsewhere in the Tanakh:

> אֶפְתְּחָה בְמָשָׁל פִּי אַבִּיעָה חִידוֹת מִנִּי־**קֶדֶם**
> *I will open my mouth with parables, I will*
> *preach with knowledge **of old.***
>
> Psalms 78:2

> יְהוָה קָנָנִי רֵאשִׁית דַּרְכּוֹ **קֶדֶם** מִפְעָלָיו מֵאָז
> *The LORD created me at the beginning of His*
> *course As the first of His works **of old.***
>
> Proverbs 8:22

According to our sages, Adonai, just as any good engineer, before creating all things, created a "scheme" to use as a basis for all of His creation. This scheme called Torah, was the oldest work of God, it was the beginning of all of His works.

> *Come and see how good is the creation of HaKadosh, Baruch Hu,*
> *His world before the creation of the world, that is, the Torah.*
>
> Midrash Mishlei 8:22

According to the words of this Psalm, we have the confirmation that Yeshua is Ben Yosef, for now we can see that the parables he told, as prophesied, were nothing more than the Torah itself by the way God determined that it should be understood and observed before the creation of all things, for the term קדם used in both passages makes the connection between the "parables" and the "Torah", thus revealing to us what Yeshua has really done, something many do not understand.

To interpret any teaching or parable of Yeshua without a deep prior knowledge of Torah is like to shoot oneself in the foot, for it is from interpretations without the Torah that idolatry is born.

* More about the parables of Yeshua in the book TORAT YEHOSHUA from the same author.

THE ANGEL
OF ISRAEL

הִנְנִי שֹׁלֵחַ מַלְאָכִי וּפִנָּה־דֶרֶךְ לְפָנָי וּפִתְאֹם יָבוֹא אֶל־הֵיכָלוֹ הָאָדוֹן | אֲשֶׁר־אַתֶּם
מְבַקְשִׁים וּמַלְאַךְ הַבְּרִית אֲשֶׁר־אַתֶּם חֲפֵצִים הִנֵּה־בָא אָמַר יְהוָה צְבָאוֹת

Behold, I am sending My messenger (angel) to clear
the way before Me, and the Lord whom you seek shall
come to His Temple suddenly. As for the angel of the
covenant that you desire, he is already coming.

Malachi 3:1

His talmidim asked him saying, why do the sages say that Eliahu
will come first? He answered them and said, indeed Eliahu will
come and will save all the world. I say to you, he has already come,
they did not know him, and they did to him according to their
desire. They will do to the son of man. Then the talmidim under-
stood that regarding Yohanan, the immerser, he was talking about.

Matthew 17:10-13

In every Pessach celebration, during the reading of the Haggadah, it is customary to leave a glass of wine on the table for
Elijah. This represents the faith and a constant desire for him
to celebrate it with us, for we would know that Mashiach Ben
David is at the door.

The relationship between Elijah and Ben David is part of
the 13 principles of the Jewish faith, because to believe in
Mashiach is also to believe in Elijah and his coming. This
relationship is mentioned in the Tanakh by the prophets, by

Yeshua, and it is something that has many mystical allegories throughout the Torah. The best known verse about both is found in the book of the prophet Malachi, which states Elijah's coming clearly and directly:

הִנֵּה אָנֹכִי שֹׁלֵחַ לָכֶם אֵת אֵלִיָּה הַנָּבִיא לִפְנֵי בּוֹא יוֹם יְהֹוָה הַגָּדוֹל וְהַנּוֹרָא

Lo, I will send the prophet Elijah to you before the coming of the awesome fearful day of Adonai.

Malachi 3:23

The relationship of both is very little studied, especially by those who believe in Yeshua, because it is already defined that Yohanan, the immerser, is Elijah. This belief causes a great void about the mysteries that this relationship has. Mashiach and Elijah belief walks side by side and that is why Yeshua had to address this idea, otherwise his proclamation of Mashiach would be inconsistent with the Tanakh.

It is written upon him that is written for my good: Behold! I am commanding my messenger (angel) to open the way before me.

Matthew 11:10

The Torah, in a very hidden way, mounts this whole scenario of Mashiach, Elijah, the land of Israel, salvation and so on. It is fascinating how one of these approaches fits with Yeshua and the Mashiach he claimed to be.

THE ANGEL

After Moses' death and before the invasion of Canaan by the People of Israel, Joshua, the current leader, sends two spies to analyze the first city to be invaded, Jericho. The first spy was called Caleb from the tribe of Judah, and the second one was called Pinchas, a member of the priestly tribe of Levi. In this infiltration, some people listened to these two men, heard what was about to happen, and because they believed in them, those people were saved.

Then appears Joshua, a leader of the tribe of Ephraim, who

invades and fights the inhabitants of those lands, establishing the land of Israel and implements the Laws of God throughout Israel.

Now let's see, let's compare this fact with Yeshua. But before that, understanding what was behind Pinchas, i.e. the angel that was upon him, is vital. A great Kabbalist sage was the first to gain this understanding through Gematria and he shows us a surprising revelation:

> *By Gematria, when you combine the name of Eliyahu Hanavi (Elijah the Prophet - 45) with the names of Adonai (72 names), we get 45 plus 72. By adding the word angel, which has a value of 91, we shall have the total value of 208, which is the same value of Pinchas' name (208).*
> Shenei Luchot Habrit, Torah Ohr

Mystically, the angel who was over Pinchas was the same angel over the prophet Elijah, so the life and mission of this spy can be seen within the missions of Elijah, which in this case, is to announce something that is about to happen and prepare those who listen to him. Rahab was one of them for example, who was warned by Pinchas about the imminent invasion of her city by the people led by Joshua.

Joshua, by leading the people, becomes the foremost man of the tribe of Ephraim, the firstborn of Yosef son of Yaakov. His genealogy is of utmost importance, for it is through it that we can fit Yeshua into this story, as well as his work and his mission. It is around this idea that the author of the book of Matthew uses some prophecy to prove what he writes.

> *In order to fulfill what was spoken by Isaiah, Behold my servant whom I have selected, my chosen one with whom my soul is pleased, I will put my spirit upon him, and he will declare justice to the nations. He will not fear nor will he run nor shall one hear him in the street. A crushed reed he will not break and a dim wick he will not quench until he establishes*

justice forever. And in his name, the gentile hope.
Matthew 12:17-21

Matthew uses a Tanakh's prophecy to prove Yeshua's messianism. The one we have above appears in Isaiah chapter 42 and this is a prophecy that generates much discord between Christians and Jews, for there are points about these verses that Yeshua apparently did not fulfill. But Matthew's intention with these Isaiah words, in this case, was not to prove the works of Yeshua, but rather who he really was and what his mission was at that particular time in history.

In order to better understand Matthew's intention, we must analyze this verse in Hebrew, for it is the only way we can see what Matthew is talking about:

הֵן עַבְדִּי אֶתְמָךְ בֹּו בְּחִירִי רָצְתָה נַפְשִׁי נָתַתִּי רוּחִי עָלָיו מִשְׁפָּט לַגּוֹיִם יוֹצִיא
This is My servant, whom I uphold, My chosen one,
in whom I delight. I have put My spirit upon him,
He shall teach the true way to the nations.
Isaiah 42:1

If we take the first words that appear in this verse and look for their numerical value, we have:

HEN AVDI ETMAKH (הן עבדי אתמך)
ך2 + מ4 + א1 + ת4 + ד4 + ב2 + ע7 + ן5 + ה5
= **8**

The number 8 is a number that represents one of the facets of Mashiach, one side of his mission in this world:

MASHIACH BEN YOSEF (משיח בן יוסף)
ף8 + ס6 + ו6 + י1 + ן5 + ב2 + ח8 + י1 + ש3 + מ4
= **8**

What we see here is the author of Matthew using a prophecy not to prove Yeshua's deeds, but to reveal the person and which mission of Mashiach Yeshua was accomplishing. This chapter of the book of Isaiah makes several allusions about Mashiach, in some verses about Mashiach Ben Yosef, in another about Mashiach Ben David, as they are all interconnected, it proves that both are the same person.

A Midrash on this verse reveals the same understanding and shows his association with the work referred to Mashiach Ben Yosef:

> *We should not be ashamed of the generation of Mashiach. The Holy One, Blessed Be He, said to them, "This is My servant, My chosen one, one who pleases my soul, and so forth" (Isaiah 42:1). At that moment, the Holy One, Blessed Be He, will tell you: "Ephraim, Mashiach, My Tzadik, I conceived you before the six days of creation. Now, my sadness is for what you will go through...*
> Midrash Psikta Rabbati 36:1

The midrash makes a direct connection between Ephraim and Mashiach, since Ephraim was the firstborn of Yosef. In several other midrashim, we see that its authors refer to Mashiach Ben Yosef by the name "Ephraim" or "son of Ephraim".

Ephraim has become a second term in reference to this facet of Mashiach, so we are able now to connect the tribe of Ephraim with the facet of Mashiach that Yeshua claimed to be, Mashiach Ben Yosef, even though he is from the tribe of Judah.

It is now possible to understand the spiritual representation that the sending of the spies has. Pinchas is sent to Canaan before Joshua comes into scene, he warns a few who listened to him about what was just about to happen and this brought salvation to those who listened to him, as in Rahab's case. Just like Yohanan, the immerser, who came before Yeshua came into scene. Yohanan, like Pinchas, warned of an imminent judgment and whoever listened to him had a chance to be saved.

Pinchas had Elijah's angel over him, the same angel that was also over Yohanan, the immerser; making him worthy to announce the coming of Mashiach, the son of Ephraim, just like Joshua, and that is why Yeshua states that "an angel" would come before him and not Elijah himself (Matt. 11:10). Just as Pinchas announced Joshua Bin Nun Ben Ephraim Ben Yosef, Yohanan announced Mashiach Ben Yosef. Both Joshua and Yeshua had the same name, YEHOSHUA; and Joshua, for being part of the tribe of Ephraim, reveals us that the mission of this angel that was over Pinchas and over Yohanan has the specific goal of announcing the arriving of a Ben Yosef.

Finally, we must observe Caleb, companion of Pinchas. Their joint mission represents the joint mission of Elijah and Mashiach, just as it happened with Yeshua and Yohanan. Not coincidentally, Pinchas was from the tribe of Levi, just as Yohanan were and Caleb from the tribe of Judah, as well as Yeshua.

This Torah account about the invasion of Jericho is an allegory of what the coming of Mashiach Ben Yosef would be like, how this coming would be announced by someone somehow represented by Pinchas. We see a person from the tribe of Levi and one from the tribe of Judah having a joint mission, and this mission was a prelude that God's Law would be "scattered" throughout the land of Israel after, just as happened after its conquest, something seeing in Yeshua's death, for it "spread" the word of God all over the world, just like Joshua did when he conquered the land.

Now, concerning Mashiach Ben David, Elijah himself will announce him, not his angel, as prophesied. If Yeshua came as Ben Yosef, when he returns as Ben David, the prophet Elijah, who was once taken to the heavens, will come first alongside with Enoch.

Now it becomes clear the verse 10 of Matthew chapter 11, where Yeshua calls "the one who will open the way before me" (see above) as an "angel", for Yohanan, the immerser, was not Elijah, but he had the same angel that was above Elijah. This is why the passage quoted above from *Shenei Luchot Habrit, Torah Ohr*, reveals the angel that was above Pinchas has the same numerical value of Elijah's name. This is one of the reasons that many jews were not able to identify Yeshua as Mashiach, for they were expecting Ben David and Elijah. Due to that leak of knowledge, they were not able to understand this angel above Yohanan.

> *My people suffer because leak of knowledge...*
>
> Hoseas 4:6a

This is the Angel of Israel.

THE LORD OF DAVID

לְדָוִד מִזְמוֹר נְאֻם יְהֹוָה | לַאדֹנִי שֵׁב לִימִינִי עַד־אָשִׁית אֹיְבֶיךָ הֲדֹם לְרַגְלֶיךָ

Of David. A psalm. The LORD said to my lord, "Sit at My right hand while I make your enemies your footstool".

Psalm 110:1

And gathered together more Pharisees and Yeshua asked them. Saying: What, in your opinion, is Mashiach? Son of whom? And they said to him, Son of David. And he said to them, As David by the Holy Ghost called him, saying: Lord. As it is written, Adonai said to my lord, Sit at my right hand and until I make your enemies the footstool of your feet. If David called him Lord, how could he then be his son? And they could not answer him a word, and since then they were afraid to ask him anything.

Matthew 22:41-46

The New Testament is not a book that should be interpreted without the Tanakh, for it is a book written by Jews, to Jews. By reading the teachings of rabbis like Yeshua and Paul, it is of the utmost importance that, in addition to a good knowledge of Torah, a deeper understanding about how was their relationship with the Torah is mandatory, for the teaching of both of them is strongly influenced by their vision about the Word of God.

One's view of the Bible is made up by two factors. The first one is something more personal, is the particular interpretation that each one of us has when we read the bible. The second one involves education, background and how the Scriptures was taught to us. The Torah, without any doubt, is the central core for these two rabbis. Their Judaism exerted enormous influence on everything they did and taught, for it was the only reality they knew, the world to them, first-century rabbis, was seen through Jewish lens. Therefore, the Oral Torah and the rabbinic mentality are the major sources that we must look at in order to understand the teachings of these two, especially those of Yeshua, who only taught for the Jews.

In these verses we have a classic case of confrontation between Yeshua and the sages. Yeshua begins by asking them who, according to their point of view, would be Mashiach. Through the answer they gave, Yeshua quotes a Psalm of David and places a question that makes them speechless. The Psalm quoted by Yeshua, according to the sages, is a Messianic Psalm where King David calls Mashiach as lord. Yeshua, clinging to that, questions the sages how could David call a descendant of his as his lord.

לְדָוִד מִזְמוֹר נְאֻם יְהֹוָה | לַאדֹנִי שֵׁב לִימִינֵי עַד־אָשִׁית אֹיְבֶיךָ הֲדֹם לְרַגְלֶיךָ

By David. A Psalm. Adonai said to my lord, "sit you at my right as I make your enemies the footstool for your feet".

Psalms 110:1

Let's look at some points in this story from the book of Matthew. The common understanding about those verses is that Yeshua was saying that he is greater than king David. However, if we pay a closer attention to Yeshua's words, unlike other occasions, he does NOT claim to be Mashiach, what he actually does is an indirect questioning without compromising himself. This alone already refutes the thesis that he was claiming to be greater than David, this is not what he was talking about. Claiming to be greater than David would be only understood by his talmidim, because only to them he said to be Mashiach up to that moment.

Secondly, every Jew knows very well that Mashiach is greater than David, if the purpose of Yeshua's question was to teach this topic, no sage would have remained without an answer. And finally, Yeshua, by the way he questioned about Mashiach, "son of whom?", he induced the Pharisees to answer something specific. Yeshua did not want to know who Mashiach was for them, but he wanted to know what was the origin of Mashiach for them. Only these topics alone annul the theological interpretation that Yeshua simply stated that he is greater than David.

The answer we need lies in two questions, why did Yeshua specifically mentioned this Psalm and what he was refuting in regard to the teachings of the sages that left them without answer?

DAVID BY THE HOLY SPIRIT

Yeshua opens his speech justifying his own questioning. He speaks of how David recognized Mashiach as his lord and this had been passed to him by the Holy Spirit. This affirmation alone could have created a lot of debates among them, since in the Tanakh, no statement appears that this recognition of Mashiach by David was given to him by the Holy Spirit. However, this was, somehow, already known by the sages. There is something in the rabbinical literature that approaches this revelation from the Holy Spirit to David in a very similar way:

> The way one talks privately with his **Lord** is an aspect of
> the **Holy Spirit**, as well as King **David**, of blessed memory,
> who had great virtues according to the book of Psalms.
> Likutey Moharan, Torah 156:1

David, when he affirms the words of Adonai in this psalm, with absolute certainty, they were revealed to him by the Holy Spirit, as well as all of his virtues which are found in the book of Psalms.

This passage from *Likutey Moharan* fits like a glove in what Yeshua said, for as soon as he said that David's revelation came from the Holy Spirit, he quotes a Psalm in the sequence. Yeshua's connection to the Oral Torah and rabbinic teachings are strikingly strong, so this statement did not cause oddities among his listeners.

A PSALM OF DAVID

Understanding why Psalm 110 is a messianic psalm can change many things about the interpretation of Yeshua's words in this case. For this, a structural analysis of the Hebrew language used in this Psalm will be necessary, as well as some comparisons with later verses of the same chapter.

One of the methods used in rabbinic exegesis is the comparison of two verses that use similar terms or words. In some cases, when this occurs, it is customary for some rabbis to separate the verse into two parts, part A and part B. Then the same thing is done with the second verse associated with the first one. Both are divided into two parts, part A and part B and then they connect the part A of the first verse with the part B of the second verse, and vice versa, and so, many hidden messages in the Tanakh are revealed.

In addition to this method, an analysis of some of the terms of this verse in its original will be required. Every Hebrew word has a root, this root usually consists of three letters, four in a few cases, and through these three letters, new words can be formed. These new words, for being from the same root as the original word, can be replaced in the verse, thus bringing a new understanding.

With this in mind, let's look at the word "my lord" which, according to the rabbis, refers to Mashiach:

לְדָוִד מִזְמוֹר נְאֻם יְהֹוָה | לַ**אדֹנִ**י שֵׁב לִימִינִי עַד־אָשִׁית אֹיְבֶיךָ הֲדֹם לְרַגְלֶיךָ

By David, a Psalm, Adonai said | To my lord (אדני): "sit you at

my right as I make your enemies the footstool for your feet".
Psalms 110:1

In this passage, the word "my lord" appears as ADONI (אדני), which is a contracted form of ADON SHELI (אדון שלי). The word ADON (אדון) - *LORD* - has the same root as DIN (דין) - *LAW* - which has the some root as the word YADIN (ידין), which is a conjugated form of the verb TO JUDGE, as it appears in Psalm 110:6:

ידין בגוים מלא גויות מחץ ראש על ארץ רבה
You will judge (YADIN) the nations, heaping up bodies
and crushing heads far and wide.

Psalms 110:6

Now we have a connection between verse 1 and verse 6, for we have a word from the same root in both of them and it is possible to divide those verses into part A and part B. The partition should be held just where the words ADONI (my lord) and YADIN (to judge) appear, because they are words of the same root.

Psalm 110:1
  ·PART A = By David, a Psalm, Adonai said to **my lord**.
  ·PART B = Sit at my right as I make your enemies the footstool of your feet.

Psalm 110:6
  ·PART A = You will **judge** the nations.
  ·PART B = Heaping up bodies and crushing heads far and wide.

By crossing between the first A and the second B and between the first B with the second A, we shall have:

1 - By David, a psalm. Adonai said to my lord: I will heap up bodies and I will crush heads far and wide.

2 – You will judge the nations, sit at my right hand while I make your enemies the footstool of your feet.

Looking at the number 1, we do not have a very weird verse, but in the case of the number 2, apparently, it completely loses its meaning. Perhaps if we look at it in Hebrew something might appear behind this crazy definition:

ידין בגוים מלא | שב לימיני עד-אשית איביך הדם לרגליש

This is the number 2 in Hebrew. If we take the first letters of the first three words (ידין בגוים מלא) from left to right we will have (מ - ב - י) representing:

מ - Mashiach - משיח
ב - Ben - בן
י - Yosef - יסף

Now we have something meaningful about what the Psalm says. If we take number 2 and replace the words, we will have the reason why this psalm is seen as a messianic psalm, as follows:

Mashiach Ben Yosef sits at my right as I make his enemies the footstool of his feet.

And verse 7 continues, confirming what we have analyzed up to now:

מִנַחַל בַּדֶּרֶךְ יִשְׁתֶּה עַל־כֵּן יָרִים רֹאשׁ
He shall drink from the stream on his way, and shall holds his head high.

Psalms 110:7

Just as before, if we take the first letters of the first three words (מ-ב-י) but from right to left this time, we shall have again:

מ - Mashiach - משיח
ב - Ben - בן

Yosef- י -יסף

Likewise, if we replace the original three words by the name of Mashiach, we will have:

Mashiach Ben Yosef shall hold his head high.

To conclude, an interrelated reading of these three verses, 1, 6 and 7, will show the true revelation of Mashiach. It is impressive:

By David, a Psalm. Adonai said: Mashiach Ben Yosef will judge the nations sitting at my right while I make his enemies the footstool of his feet, by heaping up bodies and crushing heads far and wide and Mashiach Ben Yosef will remain with head held high.

MASHIACH BEN YOSEF

So far so good, however the above psalms speak about Mashiach Ben Yosef and the book of Matthew refers to Mashiach Ben David. Some topics on Mashiach have already been set forth at the beginning of this book, but it is necessarily to go through again on some topics that might clarify what was happening between those sages and Yeshua.

Looking only at Mashiach Ben Yosef, the sages say that his main purpose is to prepare the People of Israel (we are not talking about Jews here) for redemption and to bring it to an appropriate spiritual level for the coming of Mashiach Ben David and this is only possibly through the teaching of Torah. This redemption, which can also be understood as repentance, is what will trigger the coming of Ben David, as the sages report:

"He announces salvation". It is written in the singular because it refers to Mashiach Ben Yosef.

Kol HaTor 2:81

"To bring a Redeemer" - This is the mission of Mashiach Ben Yosef

Mashiach Ben Yosef will prepare the world for the coming of Ben David. He will perform miracles, healings and wonders, he will cause strife and many wars, and will cause Edom to strike against Israel, and for this reason they will be destroyed by Mashiach Ben David. This is an interesting claim, for the term Edom in Jewish literature refers to the Christian nations, which are anti-Semitic in their essences.

Another thing we must notice about Mashiach Ben Yosef is that, in order for his work to be complete, he must first know death. We must keep in mind that we are not talking about two *Mashiachim* (plural of Mashiach), but about only one. The distinction between Ben Yosef and Ben David is given by the difference of his missions. While Ben Yosef will bring redemption to Israel and will pass through death, Ben David will bring the judgment upon the nations, will separate the good from the wicked and will reign in Jerusalem, bringing an era of peace to the world.

THE TRICKY QUESTION
When Yeshua questioned the sages, he was actually being a little tricky somehow, for he wanted to reveal, even if in a very indirect way, that his mission as Mashiach was not exactly as they expected.

If we approach to the disagreements between Yeshua and Yohanan, the immerser, we see that the vision and expectation that Yohanan had in Mashiach were not actually being "realized" by Yeshua, which generated doubts in Yohanan's mind about him, for the immerser was expecting a Ben David. This expectation was not only held by Yohanan, but also by a lot of Jews, by many of the Pharisees, by many of the rabbis and by many of the sages, for to them, Mashiach Ben Yosef had already came, as Rabbi Saadiah Gaon said:

Rabbi Gaon notes that: Joshua is Mashiach Ben Yosef, just as

Ezra and Nehemiah had the missions of Mashiach Ben Yosef.

Kol HaTor 2:116

For many of the sages, Joshua Bin Nun was Mashiach Ben Yosef and therefore the Mashiach would now have to come in the form of Ben David.

When Yeshua makes mention of this Psalm, he indirectly points out an error of interpretation in some of the Jewish exegeses. The question that makes the sages not able to answer is precisely referring to the work of Ben Yosef, works that Yeshua had been doing and the sages were not understanding. This is the reason his question caused great confusion in their minds.

The accounts of Yeshua's deeds in the book of Matthew are well compatible with the rabbinical descriptions of Mashiach Ben Yosef, his teachings, the doors opening to the gentiles, redemption, salvation, death, and bringing wars. And that's not all, but the full name of Yeshua also resembles this form os Mashiach, for he was named Yehoshua Ben Yosef.

Thus we have the answers to the initial questions, he mentioned this Psalm to reveal that the rabbinical teachings, of which Mashiach Ben Yosef had already came, were mistaken and for this reason, Yeshua wanted to show that his mission was as Ben Yosef and not as Ben David, as they expected.

ARGUMENTS

Psalm 110 is an aggregate of mystical verses, the study we have done about them reveals some things concerning the differences between Adonai and Mashiach, and the extent of his mission. The Psalm tells us that Mashiach's mission will be to judge the nations and Adonai's mission is to subdue the nations under Mashiach's feet. Mashiach, if were some sort of "god", would not need God to subdue his enemies, he would do it by himself, as well as sitting at one's own right is somewhat inexplicable.

The difference between Mashiach and God is clear, surely Mashiach has a spiritually elevated soul and a divine essence, but Adonai is God and Mashiach is Mashiach.

UNDER CURSE

וָאֹמַר אֲלֵיהֶם אִם־טוֹב בְּעֵינֵיכֶם הָבוּ שְׂכָרִי וְאִם־לֹא | חֲדָלוּ וַיִּשְׁקְלוּ אֶת־שְׂכָרִי שְׁלֹשִׁים כָּסֶף
יג וַיֹּאמֶר יְהֹוָה אֵלַי הַשְׁלִיכֵהוּ אֶל־הַיּוֹצֵר אֶדֶר הַיְקָר אֲשֶׁר יָקַרְתִּי מֵעֲלֵיהֶם וָאֶקְחָה שְׁלֹשִׁים הַכֶּסֶף וָאַשְׁלִיךְ אֹתוֹ בֵּית יְהוָה אֶל־הַיּוֹצֵר

Then I said to them, "If you are satisfied, pay me my wages; if not, don't." So they weighed out my wages, thirty shekels of silver. the noble sum that I was worth in their estimation. The LORD said to me, "Deposit it in the treasury." And I took the thirty shekels and deposited it in the treasury in the House of the LORD.
Zechariah 11:12-13

Then one of the twelve, whose name was Yehudah Eshkarioto, went to the high priest. He said, what will you give me that I should deliver Yeshua over you? They settled with him for thirty pieces of silver.
Matthew 26:14-15

According to the New Testament, the prophecy we have in the book of Zechariah is one of the most accurate, both regarding the amount for which Yeshua was betrayed, as well as the fate that was given to this money shortly after Yodeah Eshkarioto returns it to priests.

This alone makes the understanding regarding the fulfillment of this prophecy very clear and straightforward, however, the question is: what this fulfillment in the life of Yeshua actually teaches us? For this fact has no connection with his claim to be Mashiach, to be the Redeemer, nor to bring salvation to the Gentiles. Therefore, I ask, what was the relevance of this prophecy that was materialized in Yeshua and why was it important to confirm his Messianism?

To make things clearer, we must first make some connections. The amount that was paid for the head of Yeshua was thirty silver coins, or thirty Shekalim (Shekel, Israeli currency). This term, SHLOSHIM SHEKALIM (שלשים שקלים) - *thirty shekalim* - appears in a very different Torah passage and that is where we should begin:

אִם־עֶבֶד יִגַּח הַשּׁוֹר אוֹ אָמָה כֶּסֶף | **שְׁלֹשִׁים שְׁקָלִים** יִתֵּן לַאדֹנָיו וְהַשּׁוֹר יִסָּקֵל

But if the ox gores a slave, male or female, he shall pay thirty shekalim of silver to the master, and the ox shall be stoned.

Exodus 21:32

In this passage, the Torah states that if one's ox kills another man's male slave or female slave, the owner of the animal must pay the amount of thirty Shekalim to the owner of the slain slave and then, stone the ox. Despite being an obvious-looking ordinance, one of the great sages makes a very interesting comment about it:

From this we understand that the Israelites are no better than the ox they worshiped in the wilderness, placing theirselves under this curse; now their lives worth no more than thirty Shekalim.
Shenei Luchot Habrit, Torah Shebikhtav, Mishpatim, Torah Orh 86

This sage makes a somewhat strange connection between the ox that killed the slave with the ox (golden calf) that was made and worshiped shortly after the Hebrew people left Egypt. Just as the life of a slave is worth only thirty Shekalim, so is the life of the one who puts himself under the curse of idolatry.

The worship of ox images does not only occurred in the desert, but also many years after this, the people fall again under the curse of idolatry and end up worshiping another image of an ox, as stated in the book of I Kings:

Jeroboam fortified Shechem in the hill country of Ephraim and resided there; he moved out from there and fortified Peniel. Jeroboam said to himself, "Now the kingdom may well return to the House of David. If these people still go up to offer sacrifices at the House of the LORD in Jerusalem, the heart of these people will turn back to their master, King Rehoboam of Judah; they will kill me and go back to King Rehoboam of Judah." So the king took counsel and made two golden calves. He said to the people, "You have been going up to Jerusalem long enough. This is your god, O Israel, who brought you up from the land of Egypt!"
I Kings 12:25-28

After King Solomon's death, Israel was divided into two kingdoms, the Kingdom of Israel to the north under the rule of Jeroboam and the Kingdom of Yehudah to the south under the rule of Rehoboam. As the king of the north did not want his people to go to Jerusalem, he had an ox-shaped god made so that the people would worship it without leaving the lands of the Kingdom of Israel. With this, the people of the northern kingdom place themselves again under the curse of idolatry and once again with an ox shaped god.

As the story unfolds, we see numerous prophets being raised by God, such as Elijah for example, who warned the people of the Kingdom of Israel about the curse they were placing themselves under and the price that they would have to pay if they did not return to Adonai. In the end, due to the prostitution of this people with false gods, the Assyrian empire invaded Israel and spread its population to the four corners of the ancient known world, something which caused their assimilation into other gentile societies.

As mentioned above, one of Yeshua's missions is precisely to gather and bring back all the descendants of these tribes, which are scattered all over the world. Each of these people, according to our sages, has a "spark" within their souls that was given by God at the time of the deliverance of the Torah at the foot of Mount Sinai. For this mission of Yeshua to be possible, it is necessary that the curse imposed by this idolatry be first removed, and therefore, the following is reported to us by Paul, who knew all this:

> *Mashiach has redeemed us from the curse of the law, being made a curse for us: for it is written, Cursed is every one that hangs on a tree.*
>
> Galatians 3:13

Now all is clear, the passage from Exodus seen above explains why Yeshua was sold for thirty Shekalim, thus establishing a connection with Zechariah's prophecy, for it makes a direct connection between this value (thirty Shekalim) with the image of an ox that represents idolatry and its curse. So we have the answer to my question, this prophecy was given not only to make an obvious connection with Yeshua, but to show that his death on the tree, thus becoming cursed, was to precisely carry out the curse that was upon the descendants of the people of Israel, so that they may become clean and worthy again to receive the true word of God, ready to be gathered and ready to be redeemed by the redeeming work of Mashiach.

The thirty Shekalim for the sale of Yeshua serves to teach us what was the curse he carried on the tree, just as the slave is killed, Yeshua was killed, just as thirty Shekalim were to be paid, Yodeah Eshkarioto received thirty Shekalim and just like the ox had to be killed, the idolatry (ox) had to be removed (killed).

To sum up, the curse that Yeshua carried on the tree was not all curses, but the curse of idolatry that caused all the disgrace on the people of Israel.

When the high priest got the coins, he said, it is not allowed
for us to place these coins in the Temple for they are the fruit
of blood, since they were given for the blood of Yeshua. So they
took counsel and gave them for a field of a certain potter of clay
that they might put strangers there. Therefore that field is called
tent of blood unto this day. Then was fulfilled the words of
Zechariah, the prophet, and I said to them, if it is good in your
eyes, multiply my wages, but if not, forbear. So they weighed
for my wages thirty pieces of silver. Then Adonai told me, cast
it unto the potter. This is from the man who forms clay.
Matthew 27:6-9

With this you can see one more of Ben Yosef's missions, the removal of the unclean spirit, the removal of the curse of idolatry that was above his people, so that they may again become worthy of being saved by Adonai.

MY FRIEND

גַּם־אִישׁ שְׁלוֹמִי ׀ אֲשֶׁר־בָּטַחְתִּי בוֹ אוֹכֵל לַחְמִי הִגְדִּיל עָלַי עָקֵב

*My friend in whom I trusted, even he who shares
my bread, has been utterly false to me.*

Psalms 41:10

*And he answered to them: he who shall dip the Karpas in the salted
water with me, is the one who passes the information on me. And
no one could recognize him, for if they had recognized him, they
would have destroyed him. Yeshua said to them, truly the son of
man goes as it is written concerning him, woe to that man for
whose sake the son of man is betrayed. Better would be for that
man not to have been born. Yehudah, who sold him, answered
and said to him, rabbi, am I the one? He said, you have spoken.*

Matthew 26:23-25

In this psalm of David, widely used as a prophecy related to
the betrayal that Yeshua would have to go through, is part of
the extensive catalog of prophecies related to his life, messianism, person, and work. Everyone knows that Yeshua was
betrayed by one of his followers, a man named YODEAH ES-
HKARIOTO (יודא אשכריוטו), known in English as JUDAS ISCAR-
IOT.

As with all Yeshua-related prophecies, a plain look cannot
reveal the great spiritual mysteries they possess. When David
was inspired by God to compose this psalm, he was actually
revealing, in a very specific way, not only what would happen
to Yeshua, but also by whom and how.

In order for such an understanding to be possible, we must inevitably resort to Gematria, beginning with the calculation of all the letters that make up this verse of Psalm 41, which has a total value of 2157. If we use the calculation by Mishpar Katan, we have the value of 6, for 2 + 1 + 5 + 7 = 15, where 1 + 5 = **6**. Such value is already capable of revealing a very interesting name:

YODEAH ESHKARIOTO (יודא אשכריוטו)

6ו + 9ט + 6ו + 1י + 2ר + 2כ + 3ש + 1א + 1א + 4ד + 6ו + 1י

42 = 4+2 = **6**

In order to confirm what was seen above, another type of analysis fits in very well. What few know is that the whole history of humanity and the life of every servant of the Creator is already written within the words of the Torah; everything that occurred in ancient times, as well as in more modern events, is already revealed and written within the word of God. Before I continue, I would like to give an example of how this mysterious side of the Torah works.

As an example, a recent event, the World War II. All the atrocities that have occurred in it have already been revealed to us by the Torah. Let's look at some "innocent" verses found in Deuteronomy:

יְהוָה אֱלֹהֵיכֶם הְוּא אֱלֹהֵי הָאֱלֹהִים וַאֲדֹנֵי הָאֲדֹנִים הָאֵל הַגָּדֹל הַגִּבֹּר וְהַנּוֹרָא

אֲשֶׁר לֹא יִשָּׂא פָנִים וְלֹא יִקַּח שֹׁחַד

עֹשֶׂה מִשְׁפַּט יָתוֹם וְאַלְמָנָה וְאֹהֵב גֵּר לָתֶת לוֹ לֶחֶם וְשִׂמְלָה

וַאֲהַבְתֶּם אֶת־הַגֵּר כִּי־גֵרִים הֱיִיתֶם בְּאֶרֶץ מִצְרָיִם

אֶת־יְהוָה אֱלֹהֶיךָ תִּירָא אֹתוֹ תַעֲבֹד וּבוֹ תִדְבָּק וּבִשְׁמוֹ תִּשָּׁבֵעַ

הוּא תְהִלָּתְךָ וְהוּא אֱלֹהֶיךָ אֲשֶׁר־עָשָׂה אִתְּךָ אֶת־הַגְּדֹלֹת וְאֶת־הַנּוֹרָאֹת הָאֵלֶּה אֲשֶׁר רָאוּ עֵינֶיךָ

בְּשִׁבְעִים נֶפֶשׁ יָרְדוּ אֲבֹתֶיךָ מִצְרָיְמָה וְעַתָּה שָׂמְךָ

יְהוָה אֱלֹהֶיךָ כְּכוֹכְבֵי הַשָּׁמַיִם לָרֹב

*For the LORD your God is God supreme and Lord supreme, the
great, the mighty, and the awesome God, who shows no favor
and takes no bribe, but upholds the cause of the fatherless and
the widow, and befriends the stranger, providing him with
food and clothing. You too must befriend the stranger, for you
were strangers in the land of Egypt. You must revere the LORD
your God: only Him shall you worship, to Him shall you hold
fast, and by His name shall you swear. He is your glory and He
is your God, who wrought for you those marvelous, awesome
deeds that you saw with your own eyes. Your ancestors went
down to Egypt seventy persons in all; and now the LORD your
God has made you as numerous as the stars of heaven.*

Deuteronomy 10:17-22

These passages from the book of Deuteronomy send a very
strong message. From the letter HEI (ה) highlighted above, we
should count 22 letters. The 22th letter is the letter YUD (י),
22 other letters from the latter, we have the letter TAV (ט),
then 22 more we have the letter LAMED (ל) and after another
22 letters, we have the letter RESH (ר), thus forming the word
(היטלר).

The formed word (היטלר), in English, is hITLER. And it doesn't
stop there, the count is made every 22 letters, and funny or
not, in 1922 was the year hitler took over the leadership of
the Nazi party. That's not all, using the same verses, we can
see another example addressing World War II:

יְהוָה אֱלֹהֵיכֶם הוּא אֱלֹהֵי הָאֱלֹהִים וַאֲדֹנֵי הָאֲדֹנִים הָאֵל הַגָּדֹל הַגִּבֹּר וְהַנּוֹרָא
אֲשֶׁר לֹא יִשָּׂא פָנִים וְלֹא יִקַּח שֹׁחַד

עֹשֶׂה מִשְׁפַּט יָתוֹם וְאַלְמָנָה וְאֹהֵב גֵּר לָתֶת לוֹ לֶחֶם וְשִׂמְלָה
וַאֲהַבְתֶּם אֶת־הַגֵּר כִּי־גֵרִים הֱיִיתֶם בְּאֶרֶץ מִצְרָיִם

אֶת־יְהוָה אֱלֹהֶיךָ תִּירָא אֹתוֹ תַעֲבֹד וּבוֹ תִדְבָּק וּבִשְׁמוֹ תִּ**שׁ**ָּבֵעַ

הוּא תְהִלָּתְךָ וְה**וּא** אֱלֹהֶיךָ אֲשֶׁר־עָשָׂה **א**ִתְּךָ אֶת־הַגְּדֹלֹת וְאֶת־**הַ**נּוֹרָאֹת
הָאֵלֶּה אֲשֶׁר רָאוּ עֵינֶיךָ

בְּשִׁבְעִים נֶפֶשׁ יָרְדוּ אֲבֹתֶיךָ מִצְרָיְמָה וְעַתָּה שָׂמְךָ

יְהוָה אֱלֹהֶיךָ כְּכוֹכְבֵי הַשָּׁמַיִם לָרֹב

For the LORD your God is God supreme and Lord supreme, the
great, the mighty, and the awesome God, who shows no favor
and takes no bribe, but upholds the cause of the fatherless and
the widow, and befriends the stranger, providing him with
food and clothing. You too must befriend the stranger, for you
were strangers in the land of Egypt. You must revere the LORD
your God: only Him shall you worship, to Him shall you hold
fast, and by His name shall you swear. He is your glory and He
is your God, who wrought for you those marvelous, awesome
deeds that you saw with your own eyes. Your ancestors went
down to Egypt seventy persons in all; and now the LORD your
God has made you as numerous as the stars of heaven.

Deuteronomy 10:17-22

This time the count will be every 13 letters from the letter
SHIN (ש) highlighted above. In the Kabbalah 13 is a bad number, for may mean death. Counting every 13 letters, as highlighted, we will have the word SHOAH (שואה) which means
HOLOCAUST.

Fantastic revelations!

Returning to the numerical value of the verse in Psalm, the
value of 2157, we are able to find another passage from the
book of Leviticus with the same total value of 2157 by the
sum of its letters. This passage, even if has not an obvious
and direct connection with the prophetic Psalm, hides a very
iconic name in its words:

וַיָּבֹא מֹשֶׁה וְאַהֲרֹן אֶל אֹהֶל מוֹעֵד וַיֵּצְאוּ וַיְבָרֲכוּ

אֶת־הָעָם וַיֵּרָא כְבוֹד־יְהוָה אֶל־כָּל־הָעָם

Moses and Aaron then went inside the Tent of Meeting.
When they came out, they blessed the people; and the
Presence of the Lord appeared to all the people.

Leviticus 9:23

From the first letter YUD (י) appearing in this verse, a count with multiples of 6 must be made. The sixth (6x1) letter from from the first highlighted YUD (י) is the letter VAV (ו), the twelfth (6x2) letter from the VAV (ו) is the letter DALET (ד) and the twelfth (6x2) Letter counted from DALET (ד) is the letter ALEF (א).

Putting it all together, we have the word YODEAH (יודא), which in English is translated as JUDAS.

Now, why the counting is made with multiples of 6? Apart from being the value of Yodeah Eshkarioto's name (as above), the value 6 is also the value of the following words:

BEGUIDAH (בגידה) - BETRAYAL

ב2 + ג3 + י1 + ד4 + ה5

15 = 1+5 = **6**

BOGUED (בוגד) - TRAITOR

ב2 + ו6 + ג3 + ד4

15 = 1+5 = **6**

What we see here is the name of YODEAH in a not so clear way, it proves to us that everything is already revealed by the Torah. So I ask, did Yeshua have a divine revelation about who the traitor was, or was his unique knowledge of Torah good enough to show him who would betray him?

Lastly, the Tanakh not only tells who would be the traitor, but also who would be the betrayed. Looking at a second passage that deals with Yeshua's betrayal, we have the following:

וָאֹמַר אֲלֵיהֶם אִם־טוֹב בְּעֵינֵיכֶם הָבוּ שְׂכָרִי וְאִם לֹא חֲדָלוּ וַיִּשְׁקְלוּ אֶת־שְׂכָרִי שְׁלֹשִׁים כָּסֶף

וַיֹּאמֶר יְהוָה אֵלַי הַשְׁלִיכֵהוּ אֶל־הַיּוֹצֵר אֶדֶר הַיְקָר אֲשֶׁר יָקַרְתִּי מֵעֲלֵיהֶם וָאֶקְחָה שְׁלֹשִׁים הַכֶּסֶף וָאַשְׁלִיךְ אֹתוֹ בֵּית יְהוָה אֶל־הַיּוֹצֵר

Then I said to them, "If you are satisfied, pay me my wages; if not, don't." So they weighed out my wages, thirty shekels of silver. the

noble sum that I was worth in their estimation. The LORD said to me, "Deposit it in the treasury." And I took the thirty shekels and deposited it in the treasury in the House of the LORD.

Zechariah 11:12-13

From the first letter YUD (י) highlighted above, from right to left and every 24 (6x4) letters, we have a SHIN (ש), a VAV (ו) and finally an AYN (ע) - forming the word YESHUA (ישוע). Thus we understand that it was revealed that YODEAH would betray YESHUA for thirty shekalim many years before the fact.

Another proof? Let's go back to Psalm 41; David talks again about betrayal and enemies plotting against him. Two verses above the analyzed Psalm, we have one verse that fits perfectly with what happened between Yodeah, the priests, and Yeshua:

יַחַד עָלַי יִתְלַחֲשׁוּ כָּל־שֹׂנְאָי עָלַי | יַחְשְׁבוּ רָעָה לִי

All my enemies whisper together against me, imagining the worst for me.

Psalm 41:8

In the phrase "worst for **me**" (יחשבו רעה לי), counting every two letters, shows who would this "me" be; according to the letters highlighted above, it is no other than YESHUA (ישוע) himself.

Everything is in the Torah, it is up to us to study and live it, for it is the ONLY TRUTH.

SMITE THE SHEPHERD

חֶרֶב עוּרִי עַל־רֹעִי וְעַל־גֶּבֶר עֲמִיתִי נְאֻם יְהוָה צְבָאוֹת הַךְ
אֶת־הָרֹעֶה וּתְפוּצֶיןָ הַצֹּאן וַהֲשִׁבֹתִי יָדִי עַל־הַצֹּעֲרִים

O sword! Rouse yourself against My shepherd, The man
in charge of My flock, says the LORD of Hosts. Smite
the shepherd And let the flock scatter; And I will also
turn My hand Against all the shepherd boys.

Zechariah 13:7

Then Yeshua said to his talmidim, come, all of you, be
grieved because of me tonight as it is written, smite
the shepherd and the sheep will be scattered.

Matthew 26:31

Surely all this was done because the writings of the prophets
were being fulfilled. Then all talmidim left him and fled.

Matthew 26:56

There are several terms in this prophecy that show what the
prophet Zechariah is talking about. I will highlight and analyze one by one, and then I will parallel them with other
Hebrew terms that have the same numerical value, thus being
able to substitute them:

CHEREV (חרב) - SWORD
ח8 + ר200 + ב2
= **210**

DOR (דור) - GENERATION

ד4 + ו6 + ר200

= **210**

ROE SHELI (רעי = רעה שלי) - MY SHEPHERD

ר2 + ע7 + ה5 + ש3 + ל3 + י1

= **21**

YOSEF (יוסף)

י1 + ו6 + ס60 + ף8

= **21**

GEVER (גבר) - MAN

ג3 + ב2 + ר2

= **7**

MASHIACH (משיח)

מ4 + ש3 + י1 + ח8

16 = 1+6 = **7**

CHAKH ET HAROE (הך את הרעה) - SMITE THE SHEPHERD

ה5 + ך2 + א1 + ת4 + ה5 + ר2 + ע7 + ה5

31 = 3+1 = **4**

L'SGUIDAH (לסגידה) - DUE TO THE IDOLATRY

ל3 + ס60 + ג3 + י1 + ד4 + ה5

22 = 2+2 = **4**

HATZOEN (הצאן) - FLOCK

ה5 + צ9 + א1 + ן5

= **20**

HAISRAELIM (הישראלים) - THE ISRAELIS

ה5 + י1 + ש3 + ר2 + א1 + ל3 + י1 + ם4

= **20**

*Haisraelim (הישראלים), or Israelis, are the natural people from the State of Israel, but it is also the term used to address people from the northern kingdom, whose descendants are scattered among the nations.

TZOARIM (צערים) - BOYS / YOUNGS
צ9 + ע7 + ר2 + י1 + ם40

23 = 2+3 = **5**

GOYIM (גוים) - GENTILES
ג3 + ו6 + י1 + ם40

14 = 1+4 = **5**

השבתי

HASHVTI - Translated as "scatter" - comes from the verb LE-HASHVIT, conjugated in the first person of the past, but if we read these word as HESHAVTI (same writing), we would have a word from the verb LEHASHIV, that means "to return some-thing".

I now propose a different reading of this prophecy:

FROM THE GENERATION OF YOSEF ROUSE MY MASHIACH (MASHIACH BEN YOSEF), THE MAN IN CHARGE OF MY PEOPLE - SAYS THE LORD OF HOSTS, DUE TO THE IDOLATRY, THE ISRAELIS (KINGDOM OF ISRAEL) SPREAD, BUT I WILL RETURN THEM WITH MY HANDS FROM THE GENTILES.
Zechariah 13:7 - rereading

This is confirmed by the prophet Ezekiel:

And you, O mortal, take a stick and write on it, "Of Judah and the Israelites associated with him"; and take another stick and write on it, "Of Joseph—the stick of Ephraim and all the House of Israel associated with him". Bring them close to each other, so that they become one stick, joined together in your hand. And when any of your people ask you, "Won't you tell us what these actions of yours mean?" Answer them, "Thus said the Lord GOD: I am going to take the stick of Joseph, which is

in the hand of Ephraim and of the tribes of Israel associated
with him, and I will place the stick of Judah upon it and make
them into one stick; they shall be joined in My hand."

Ezekiel 37:16-19

THE DEATH OF MASHIACH BEN YOSEF

There is something very important to consider, the death of Mashiach Ben Yosef. According to our sages, if the people of Israel are not worthy when Mashiach Ben Yosef comes, he will come riding a donkey and will suffer the pain of a violent death. Throughout rabbinic literature, there are many commentaries and teachings regarding both the death of Mashiach Ben Yosef and the need for it to occur for the coming of Mashiach Ben David to become possible:

We know that the first Mashiach will come from
Yosef, who will die when he reveals who he is and
then will come Mashiach Ben David.

Or HaChaim, Leviticus 14:9:6

Mashiach Ben Yosef, the Mashiach who will die before
the advent of Mashiach Ben David the Redeemer.

Kedushat Levi, Bereshit, Toldot 22

Mashiach Ben Yosef was slain for the redemption
of Mashiach Ben David.

Talmud of Babylon, Tractate Sukkah 52a

As already mentioned, both Ben David and Ben Yosef are the same person, but two facets that represent different times and missions. The death of Yeshua makes complete sense with what the sages expected and it was through it that the word of God reached all nations; such feat was the beginning of the redemptive work of Mashiach Ben David.

An archaeologist find dating from around 110 b.c.e. Found in the Dead Sea and titled as *Dead Sea Stone Manuscript*, says that after the death of Mashiach Ben Yosef, he would be the first to be resurrected within a short time after his death, such expectation was also met by Yeshua.

Certainly, the "Smite the shepherd" refers to the death of Yeshua and "the scattered flock" refers to the people of Israel, people who, according to the prophets Isaiah and Ezekiel, will be gathered again thanks to this fact, to this sacrifice made by Ben Yosef.

YESHUA x jesus

According to my point of view, this prophecy of Zechariah has a negative facet, that is, it deals with a bad theme and for this reason, I cannot disassociate it from one of the foundations of the Christian faith, the trinity. The trinity is the basis of the church's faith, of course not all branches of Christianity believe in it, but the vast majority of Christians certainly hold to this doctrine not found in the bible.

The purpose of this book is not to delve into this theme, but there are some things about Trinitarianism that I would like to address First, it is clear that such a theology is a human interpretation that was born alongside with the ancient church, an idea made up by men who came from a pagan background.

In order to understand the rabbinic interpretation of this prophecy, we need a quick analysis of the ancient religions. With a simple look on them, one shall see that in all of them the trinity existed in some way. This concept had its beginning after the construction of the tower of Babel, being nimrod the first representation of the "highest" god, semiramis, the mother of nimrod was the second goddess and also mother of his son, tamuz, the god son. Upon this belief the Greek trinity was created, composed of zeus, the god father, ares the god son and hera, the spirit goddess. In Nordic we have odin as god father, thor as god son and freya as god spirit. In Egyptian, osiris is the father, horus the son and isis the spirit. In Hinduism, brahma is the father, vishnu the son and shiva the spirit, and in the Roman, jupiter is the father, mars the son and quirinus the conciliatory spirit between men and the pantheon.

The strong connection that Christianity has in its essence with the ancient pagan religions, which only changed their names, is undeniable. In the case of the church, the closest was the Roman pantheon. If we make a parallel between the Christian jesus and the god son mars, we can see some similarities:

Mars was the god of war, the god of violence and with this in mind, I dare to ask, how many war have ever been fought in the name of this Christian jesus? Crusades, inquisition, the 7 years war, second war, polgrom, among many others. We must bear in mind that the jesus christ that I am talking about now is not the same as Yeshua HaMashiach, both are different figures, one was a rabbi, Pharisee, Mashiach and a Torah teacher, the other in turn is a mythical being who presents himself as god, who freed his followers from God's will and gave them authority for a life under the rules of a Christian Puritanism that has nothing to do with the holiness required by the Creator.

With this in mind, an understanding of this "sword" that the prophet mentions in his prophecy becomes easier. A comment from one of the greatest sages clarifies and confirms all this seen so far:

> *Sword - represents the wars that will take place after the death of Mashiach Ben Yosef caused by the Gentiles.*
> Ibn Ezra, Zechariah 13:7

Ibn Ezra, a non-messianic rabbi, claims that the death of Mashiach Ben Yosef, which was one of the facets of Yeshua, would bring much "sword" to the world, such a violence that was known in the Roman world as the work of mars and so it happened and happens.

By this we understand that this prophecy does not only reveal who is Mashiach Ben Yosef and his redemptive work on the people of Israel, but it also reveals about the mythical being that would be created based on a poor understanding about who Yeshua truly was, a revelation gave by the simple word "sword".

Whoever has wisdom, understands it.

The trinity and the mythical figure created based on Yeshua are themes I deal with more clearly in another book.

A SHE-ASS AND A WEIRD PROPHECY

גֵּוִי נָתַתִּי לְמַכִּים וּלְחָיַי לְמֹרְטִים פָּנַי לֹא הִסְתַּרְתִּי מִכְּלִמּוֹת וָרֹק

I offered my back to the floggers, And my cheeks to those who plucked out my hair. I did not hide my face From insult and spittle.
Isaiah 50:6

Then they spit in his face and struck him on the back, and others slapped him in the face.
Matthew 26:67

At first, these words from the prophet Isaiah are about himself and not a prophecy concerning Mashiach. The prophet speaks about the pain and cravings he had to go through in the name of what God revealed to him, for if we take a look at his history, we shall see that Isaiah suffered great rejection and persecution within Israel because of what he prophesied, prophecies that led him to a violent death.

However, we also see a similar suffering that happened to Yeshua, which has led many interpreters to associate these words with the gospel accounts due to the similarities of terms used by both the authors, thus making it a kind of prophecy about what would happen to Yeshua, corroborating even more with what he claimed to be, the Mashiach. One thing that strikes me very much about the association of this verse with Mashiach's suffering is that this association is also made within Jewish teachings, as we can see in the following commentary:

The whole generation of Isaiah struck him in the face, plucked out his hair, and spit at him, for he was a great prophet in Israel. This is because his faith was in the coming of Mashiach.
Abarbanel, Isaiah 50:6

According to Abarbanel, there is indeed a link between Isaiah's suffering and the coming of Mashiach, for he links the suffering that Isaiah endured with the hope he had at the coming of the redeemer. However, the real interesting thing about this verse from Isaiah is its Gematria-made connection that directly links it with a quick passage from the Torah. Isaiah 50:6 total sum of its letters is equal to 3500 and this is the same as the following verse:

עִזִּים מָאתַיִם וּתְיָשִׁים עֶשְׂרִים רְחֵלִים מָאתַיִם וְאֵילִים עֶשְׂרִים
*200 **she-asses** and 20 he-goats; 200 ewes and 20 rams.*
Genesis 32:15

This verse from the book of Genesis gives the impression of an informational passage only, but it has a strong connection to something prophesied by another prophet, the prophet Zechariah. Before I start, I will first bring up a commentary concerning this verse above from one of the greatest sages who ever lived, Rabbi Bahya:

By placing the she-asses and the goats last in that order, Yaakov hinted that in the distant future Esau's descendants would be the victims of the Jewish Mashiach, who would appear riding a she-ass. We find the following verse in Zechariah 9:9 regarding this future event: Rejoice greatly, O daughter of Zion; rejoice, O daughter of Jerusalem; behold, your king shall come to you, righteous and savior, poor, riding on a she-ass, and on a donkey, the son of a she-ass. May we live the victory of Mashiach.
Rabbeinu Bahya, Genesis 32:15

In a deep and inexplicable way, Rabbi Bahya teaches us that in

Genesis 32:15, which tells the story of the reunion between Yaakov and Esau, his brother, Yaakov sends a message to Esau's descendants through the way he, Yaakov, presents his gifts to his brother, as seen above. What we see here is the real reason why Yeshua entered Jerusalem riding a she-ass, it was not to fulfill a prophecy, but rather to send a message, a message to the pagan peoples. According to Bahya, this is a message for them to prepare themselves, because it is hidden in the way the donkeys and goats were placed, as related in the verse of Genesis, that all pagans will succumb under the feet of Mashiach.

This prophecy of Isaiah is clearly associated with another prophecy fulfilled by Yeshua:

גִּילִי מְאֹד בַּת־צִיּוֹן הָרִיעִי בַּת יְרוּשָׁלַם הִנֵּה מַלְכֵּךְ יָבוֹא לָךְ צַדִּיק
וְנוֹשָׁע הוּא עָנִי וְרֹכֵב עַל־חֲמוֹר וְעַל־עַיִר בֶּן־אֲתֹנוֹת

Rejoice greatly, Fair Zion; Raise a shout, Fair Jerusalem! Lo, your king is coming to you. He is victorious, triumphant, Yet humble, riding on an ass, On a donkey foaled by a she-ass.
Zechariah 9:9

They brought the she-ass and the colt, and Yeshua rode upon it while the others placed their garments and clothes upon them. Then they made the ascent.
Matthew 21:7

The prophecy concerning Yeshua's triumphant entry into Jerusalem sitting on a she-ass is widely known, and its unlikely fulfillment is what makes it a concrete prophecy about the messianism of Yeshua's mission. However, like all words that come out from the mouths of the prophets, it must not only be understood in its literal form. What was revealed to the prophet Zechariah goes far beyond a triumphal entry and a she-ass riding, this revelation confirms to us all that has been studied about the prophecies uttered by Isaiah up to now, namely the true facet of Yeshua and his mission as Mashiach.

In Hebrew, the way the verse begins is unusual, so in its first four words we have the following:

גִּילִי **מְאֹד בַּ**ת צִ**יּ**וֹן

When we take the first letter MEM (מ) and from it we count three more letters, we will have the letter BET (ב), when we count three more letters we will have the letter YUD (י) and this shows us who the prophecy deals with:

Mashiach - מ - משיח

Ben - ב- |בן

Yosef - י - |סף

This confirms the above and why the gospels used these prophecies in reference to Yeshua, for they deal with MASHIACH BEN YOSEF. Now the question is, why did I count three letters and not four or five? Because the number three is the spiritual kabbalistic number attached to Yosef:

YOSEF (יוסף)

6ף + 6ס + 6ו + 1י

= **3**

Finally, two great sages commentaries about this prophecy. Based on them, we will have confirmation of everything seen so far:

Some say this is Mashiach Ben David, but Rabbi Moshe HaCohen says this is about Mashiach Ben Yosef that Zechariah deals with.
Ibn Ezra, Zechariah 9:9

And the prophet now saw Mashiach and God showed him how he would come to save Israel. By his righteousness he would come as poor (Ben Yosef), but he will become a rich and strong-hearted king (Ben David) and the she-ass will become like a horse ready to go to war.
Malbim, Zechariah 9:9

To sum up, Isaiah's prophecy, which relates the suffering they both went through, actually deals with the judgment that Mashiach will bring upon the pagan nations. This is also seen in the rabbinical commentaries mentioned above, which reveal what the sages' understanding about this prophecy is, an understanding that connects Isaiah's words with the prophecy of Zachariah's she-ass, something that is directly related to Yeshua and Mashiach Ben Yosef and for this reason, he fulfilled that prophecy.

Thus we understand that Yeshua, as Ben Yosef, brought to the nations the knowledge about the Living God and His Word; and alongside with this knowledge, judgment also came and no one has excuses now. All of this are found in the prophecies seen in this chapter, but not easy to understand.

DEATH, SALVATION AND ISRAEL

וְהָיָה | בַּיֹּום הַהוּא נְאֻם אֲדֹנָי יְהוִֹה וְהֵבֵאתִי הַשֶּׁמֶשׁ
בַּצָּהֳרָיִם וְהַחֲשַׁכְתִּי לָאָרֶץ בְּיֹום אֹור

*And in that day, declares my Lord GOD, I will make the sun
set at noon, I will darken the earth in the day of light.*

Amos 8:9

*At the sixth hour, darkness came in all the world
and it remained until the ninth hour.*

Matthew 27:45

Here we have something related to the death of Yeshua. The sixth hour, as reported by the book of Matthew, according to the Jewish hour count, refers to noon, just as prophesied by Amos. Many understand that at this time a solar eclipse occurred, which caused a natural darkness. But eclipse or not, the fact is that the day darkened as prophesied, and that fact was certainly not just for the fulfillment of a prophecy.

The most relevant thing about this prophecy is not the accuracy concerning the hours of the day, but it is a term used in it. In the words of the prophet does not appear to darken a day, but rather to darken a very specific day, a day called by the prophet as "day of light". This day of light is explained neither by the prophet nor by Matthew, and the question remains, what would this day of light be?

The reference we have in Amos 8:9 about the darkness

to come, is the weeping that our festivals will become
and our praises in vain words. But when the day of light
gets dark, it represents a new dawn, a fresh start.

Rabbeinu Chananel, Genesis 50:10

According to our sages, the day of light that will darken means the moment when the biblical feasts and biblical praises will become weeping and vain things, that is, they will lose their value among the people, the Torah will no longer be observed and the divine Laws forgotten.

כִּי לֹא מוּעָף לַאֲשֶׁר מוּצָק לָהּ כָּעֵת הָרִאשׁוֹן הֵקַל אַרְצָה זְבֻלוּן וְאַרְצָה
נַפְתָּלִי וְהָאַחֲרוֹן הִכְבִּיד דֶּרֶךְ הַיָּם עֵבֶר הַיַּרְדֵּן גְּלִיל הַגּוֹיִם

Nevertheless the land that was distressed, will not be darkened,
when at the first he lightly afflicted the land of Zebulun and the
land of Naphtali, and afterward did more grievously afflict her
by the way of the sea, beyond Jordan, in Galilee of the nations.

Isaiah 8:23

Every prophecy concerning the destruction of the Kingdom of Israel and the dispersal of its population reports a darkness that would come upon it, a population that once knew the true God, His Torah, His truth and is now scattered and absorbed by nations of pagan creeds. This makes perfect sense with the above understanding concerning this "day of light", for the festivals, praises and the Torah have been forgotten within these people, they darkened.

In verse 23 of Isaiah 8, the prophet quotes two tribes, Zebulon and Naphtali, tribes that were part of the Kingdom of Israel and were scattered throughout the world. This confirms that the day of light, which Amos refers to, is the epoch of the existence of the Kingdom of Israel, the darkness that came upon that day refers to the Assyrian invasion and the destruction of this kingdom, that caused a "forgetfulness" of God and of the Torah by this people.

With this, it is possible to connect the prophecy fulfilled in the death of Yeshua as a direct reference to one of his missions, the rescue of the people of Israel, the mission he has to return to the light their descendants, as also prophesied:

הָעָם הַהֹלְכִים בַּחֹשֶׁךְ רָאוּ אֹור גָּדֹול אֹור יֹשְׁבֵי בְּאֶרֶץ צַלְמָוֶת אֹור נָגַהּ עֲלֵיהֶם

The people that walked in darkness Have seen a brilliant light;
On those who dwelt in a land of gloom Light has dawned.

Isaiah 9:1

After the fall of what Assyria did, there will be no lost Israeli
who will be in the dark and then, they will see the great light.

Malbim, Isaiah 9:1

The death of Yeshua brought the knowledge of the God Most High and His Torah to all the world, nations and creeds, in which the descendants of these tribes find themselves; even if they do not know who they really are, as the time of Mashiach Ben David approaches, a great worldwide raising for the Torah will occur, this people, for no reason and without understanding why, will begin to seek and live Torah, people of different faiths and nationalities; for this is the accomplishment of the work of Ben Yosef, the work of gathering these tribes under the Torah and preparing these people to serve him when he comes as Ben David.

Rabbi Eliezer says: just as the day is followed by darkness and
then the light returns, so too, even if it becomes darkness for
the lost tribes, God will definitely bring them out of darkness.

Talmud of Babylon, tractate Sanhedrin 110b

When this happens, the light that will be upon these tribes, upon this people, will be much greater than the light that was upon them before the dispersion, as our sages teach:

Another interpretation that we have for "day of light"
is a rainy day. Whenever the word OR (light) appears
in the book of Job, it refers to rain, which is the source
of light that brings prosperity to man's life, for the

brightness of light is much greater after a storm.
Haamek Sheilah on Sheiltot, Part 1, 8:6

The raising of these descendants among the Gentiles and the glory of the Torah that will be seen among them will be so great that it will border on how the Torah must really be lived, they will overcome the connection that the Jews have with the Torah, for it will be much closer to what was taught and preached by Mashiach Ben Yosef; it will be a Torah unconnected with religions and dogmas, for it will be lived from the heart, because the awakening of these people will be through by the love they will have in their hearts for the Word of God and His will, something inexplicable and caused by the divine spark that each of those descendents has within, a spark placed by God at the time of the giving of the Torah on Mount Sign and passed down from generation to generation by all those who were there, and that includes all descendants of the 12 tribes, scattered or not. This concept explains a prophecy from the book of Haggai:

גָּדוֹל יִהְיֶה כְּבוֹד הַבַּיִת הַזֶּה הָאַחֲרוֹן מִן־הָרִאשׁוֹן אָמַר יְהוָה
צְבָאוֹת וּבַמָּקוֹם הַזֶּה אֶתֵּן שָׁלוֹם נְאֻם יְהוָה צְבָאוֹת

The glory of this latter House shall be greater than that of
the former one, said the LORD of Hosts; and in this place
I will grant prosperity, declares the LORD of Hosts.
Haggai 2:9

This house, where the glory will be greater in its second form, refers to the Kingdom of Israel, for this second glory will be detached from theology and creeds and will be a glory that will bring Mashiach Ben David.

And Yeshua said to them, I was not sent except to
the lost sheep of the house of Israel.
Matthew 15:24

To make this even more interesting, we have the total value of this dark verse from the book of Amos of 3034. The Sum of each number of this total (3 + 0 + 3 + 4) is equal to 10. The number 10 represents two things:

MASHIACH BEN DAVID (משיח בן דוד)
4ד+ 6ן + 4ד + 50ן + 2ב + 8ח + 10י + 300ש + 40מ
$$424 = 4+2+2 = \mathbf{10}$$

ISRAEL (ישראל)
30ל + 1א + 200ר + 300ש + 10י
$$541 = 5+4+1 = \mathbf{10}$$

Yeshua's death is more related to Mashiach Ben David than to Mashiach Ben Yosef, because it was through it that darkness above the lost sheep of Israel shall come to an end. When that happens, Ben David will come, that is, the death of Yeshua Ben Yosef was the beginning of the preparation for the coming of Yeshua Ben David, for it is through that sacrifice that God's people who is scattered among the nations will be gathered again under His will.

Now, continuing the approach on Amos's prophetic verse, the sum of its letter's will bring even more striking revelations about the whole work of Yeshua.

The sum of all the letters that compose the verse 9 from Amos chapter 8 is equal to 3034. By divine wisdom it is possible to find SIX other passages that also have the the sums of their letter equal to 3034, thus being associated with this verse. They are: *Genesis 47:31 - I Kings 11:42 - II Samuel 3:32 - Exodus 16:34 - II Kings 10:13 - Jeremiah 37:9.*

A) OBJECT OF SALVATION (3034)

וַיֹּאמֶר הִשָּׁבְעָה לִי וַיִּשָּׁבַע לֹו וַיִּשְׁתַּחוּ יִשְׂרָאֵל עַל־רֹאשׁ הַמִּטָּה
And he said, "Swear to me." And he swore to him.
Then Israel bowed at the head of the bed.

Genesis 47:31

In the last verse of chapter 47 in the book of Genesis, we see Yaakov's last words and wish. He makes his last request, so that his remains be buried in the land of Israel, in this way, Yaakov, also known as Israel, found his peace.

Although it is a passage that has no direct reference to the dispersion of the tribes of Israel, there are some points to consider. The first is that Yaakov, in this case Israel, express his wish to be taken back from a pagan nation (Egypt) to the land of Israel, to Tzion. This idea makes total sense with one of Ben Yosef's missions, which is to bring back Israel from pagan nations, that is, the descendants of the Kingdom of Israel back to the land of Israel.

Another secret found in this passage goes hand in hand with the following teaching found in the book of Acts:

> *Neither is there **salvation** in any other: for there is none other **name** under heaven given among men, whereby we must **be saved**.*
> Acts 4:12

Interestingly, the author of the book of Acts associates salvation with a name, in this case, his talking about the name of YEHOSHUA, or YESHUA in its abbreviation. Now let us look once again at the verse about Yaakov with attention to a few letters:

וַיֹּאמֶר הִשָּׁבְעָה לִי וַיִּשָּׁבַע לוֹ וַיִּשְׁתַּחוּ יִשְׂרָאֵל עַל־רֹאשׁ הַמִּטָּה
Genesis 47:31

Three times in a row the letters YUD (י), SHIN (שׁ), and AYIN (ע) appear. These three letters form the roots of the words YEHOSHUA (יהושע) - *Joshua* - YESHUAH (ישועה) - *salvation* - the verb LEHOSHIA (להושיע) - *to save* - as well as the name of YESHUA (ישוע).

To sum up, it all started with the verse of Amos about Yeshua's death, a verse that has the same numerical value as Genesis 47:31, which speak about the return of Yaakov (Israel) to the land of Israel. In this verse, the name of Yeshua is found, thus showing to us where the author of the book of Acts got this idea that connects name and salvation from. So, what we have here is that the verse of Amos also speaks about Yaakov, father of Yosef, tribe of which is associated with Mashiach Ben Yosef; it also speaks about Israel and the land of Israel, it reveals the name of Mashiach and it speaks about salvation, for all of this represents the removal of the DARKNESS that came over the world, its all connected, this is the "day of light".

This also seen in a verse somewhere else:

אַל־תִּירְאִי תּוֹלַעַת יַעֲקֹב מְתֵי יִשְׂרָאֵל אֲנִי עֲזַרְתִּיךְ
נְאֻם־יְהוָה וְגֹאֲלֵךְ קְדוֹשׁ יִשְׂרָאֵל

*Fear not, O worm **Yaakov**, O men of **Israel**: I will save you ,*
*declares Adonai. I, your **savior**, the Holy One of Israel.*

Isaiah 41:14

God delivered Yeshua so that through his death, the Holy One of Israel would reach His lost and scattered people across the nations. The death of Mashiach Ben Yosef was the fulfillment of the promise of salvation of the tribe of Israel.

That is the true object of salvation, Israel.

B) THE ESTABLISHMENT OF SALVATION (3034)

וְהַיָּמִים אֲשֶׁר מָלַךְ שְׁלֹמֹה בִירוּשָׁלַ‍ִם עַל־כָּל־יִשְׂרָאֵל אַרְבָּעִים שָׁנָה

The length of king Solomon's reign in Jerusalem,
over all Israel, was forty years.

I Kings 11:42

After King Solomon's death, the history of Israel as a nation began to have a chaotic unfolding. His descendants did not agree about who should rise to the throne and this caused a division of the tribes into two kingdoms, the Kingdom of Israel to the north, which had 10 of the 12 tribes and the Kingdom of Judah to the south, formed by the remaining 2 tribes.

King Solomon passed away around the year 932 b.c.e. and two years later, both the Northern Kingdom and the Southern Kingdom were established. Shortly after the creation of the Kingdom of Israel, its king, Yeroboham, builds the kingdom's capital, the city of Shechem, within the territory of the tribe of Efrayim, a tribe which is directly linked to Mashiach Ben Yosef.

In order for the Northern Kingdom to stand against the Southern Kingdom, King Yeroboham decides to build a new temple so that his people do not have to go to Jerusalem to sacrifice. The completion of this Temple took place around the year 921 b.c.e. about 11 years after King Solomon's death and the beginning of the division of Israel.

So, here we see that the greatest sin, the error that led the Kingdom of Israel to scatter, was the idolatry that began 11 years after Solomon's death, something mentioned by the verse above. Thus we understand that the first mission of Mashiach Ben Yosef originated just as the Northern Kingdom established a new temple and led its people to pagan practices. The number 11 has a very negative connotation, in this case, while it represents the time between Solomon's death and the beginning of Israel's error, it also reveals God's plan in this verse.

In I Kings 11:42 we find the letters MEM (מ / ם), BET (ב), YUD (י) separated exactly by 10 letters between each, that is, from the first MEM (ם), with a count of 11 letters, we have BET (ב) and 11 more, we have YUD (י) - forming the initials of MASHI-ACH (משיח) BEN (בן) YOSEF (יוסף):

וְהַיָּמִ֗**ם** אֲשֶׁר֩ מָלַ֨ךְ שְׁלֹמֹ֤ה **ב**ִירוּשָׁלַ֙**ם** **על** כָּל **י**ִשְׂרָאֵ֖ל אַרְבָּעִ֥ים שָׁנָֽה
I Kings 11:42

One of the reasons this facet of Mashiach is related to the tribe of Efrayim, besides the high resemblance his mission bears to

Yosef's life, is that it was in these lands that the idolatry that destroyed Israel began 11 years after the end of Solomon's reign. So, in the same verse we can kinda see the mission of Mashiach Ben Yosef and understand that it only began to take place after the death of Yeshua, for it is a verse that has the same numerical value as the passage of Amos that prophesies his death has.

In this verse of I Kings, reveals to us who's death the prophet Amos is talking about. In the term "in Jerusalem" (בירושלם על), every three letters we find an important root:

$$\text{בי}\textbf{רוש}\text{לם על}$$

YUD (י) - SHIN (ש) - AYIN (ע) - which form both the verb "to save" - lehoshia (להושיע) - as well as the root of the name of Yeshua (ישוע).

We learn here that the prophecy of Amos is not actually talking about a darkness that would come over the world, but it is revealing why this darkness came. He reveals that after the death of King Solomon, the mission of Mashiach Ben Yosef to save the tribes of Israel began; mission which would be formalized with his death and fully realized with his return; this is why the darkness came, it came as a sign of the beginning of the completion of this particular mission of his, to take the Torah back to his lost sheep and when it happens, we shall see the "day of light".

C) THE ORIGIN OF SALVATION (3034)

וַיִּקְבְּרוּ אֶת־אַבְנֵר בְּחֶבְרוֹן וַיִּשָּׂא הַמֶּלֶךְ אֶת־קוֹלוֹ
וַיֵּבְךְּ אֶל־קֶבֶר אַבְנֵר וַיִּבְכּוּ כָּל־הָעָם

And so they buried Abner at Hebron; the king wept
aloud by Abner's grave, and all the troops wept.

II Samuel 3:32

Our sages teach that each verse from the Tanakh has 77 different understandings hidden in its words. Such a statement I truly believe, especially when I come across a verse that has no connection with the subject I am studying, a verse that deals with a completely adverse subject. Every time this happens, my level of faith increases, for wisdom, knowledge, and understanding come only from one source, God.

Salvation, death, Israel, nothing addressed up to now makes sense with this verse, however, the verse has the same numerical value as the verse of Amos' prophecy. Due to this fact, this verse strangely must also address the subject of this study seen so far, we just have to know how to see it. The words from Samuel has a hidden prophecy in it, a prophecy that speaks about the origin of where this salvation would come from, the origin of one who would die for that salvation to take place; a simple message but hard to see.

In the verse of II Samuel, in Hebrew, we must highlight each first letter of each word contained in it, thus, by the Gematria of these letters, a slight reference about Yeshua is revealed:

$$\text{וַיִּקְבְּרוּ אֶת אַבְנֵר בְּחֶבְרוֹן וַיִּשָּׂא הַמֶּלֶךְ אֶת קוֹלוֹ}$$
$$\text{וַיֵּבְךְּ אֶל קֶבֶר אַבְנֵר וַיִּבְכּוּ כָּל הָעָם}$$
$$61 + 1ק + 1א + 5ה + 61 + 2ב + 1א + 1א + 61$$
$$5ה + 2כ + 61 + 1א + 1ק + 1א +$$
$$=45$$

The number 45 has a strong connection with the land of Nazareth. For this to make sense, we must look at another prophecy found in the book of Matthew that talks about this city:

He came and dwelt in a city called Notzeret (Nazareth), in order to fulfill what the prophet said, he shall be called Notzrit (Nazarene).
Matthew 2:23

Many claim that the prophecy mentioned in the book of Matthew is not found in the Tanakh, for through all its books, the word "Nazarene" does not appear; but with a careful analysis of what Isaiah says, we will see where Matthew got it from.

וְיָצָא חֹטֶר מִגֵּזַע יִשָׁי **וְנֵצֶר** מִשָּׁרָשָׁיו יִפְרֶה
But a shoot shall grow out of the stump of Jesse,
*from a **twig** shall sprout salvation.*

Isaiah 11:1

The term that appears as "twig" in Isaiah is NETZER (נצר), this is a word that has a root formed by the letters NUN (נ), TZADIK (צ) and RESH (ר), letters which also form the word NOTZERET (נצרת) - NAZARETH or NAZARENE.

So, we can then read the verse from Isaiah as follows:

But a shoot shall grow out of the seed of Yesse (David),
from NAZARETH shall sprout salvation.
Isaiah 11: 1 - rereading

The term "salvation will come from Nazareth" would be ME-NOTZERET HAYESHUAH (מנצרת הישעה). The word YESHUAH in this case is the term for salvation in Hebrew and not the name of YESHUA. By Gematria we will have:

MENOTZERET HAYESHUAH (מנצרת הישעה)
מ4 + נ5 + צ9 + ר2 + ת4 + ה5 + י1 + ש3 + ע7 + ה5
= **45**

This tells us that Amos's prophecy about the death of Yeshua also revealed where the one who would die for Israel would come from.

D) THE OIL OF SALVATION (3034)

כַּאֲשֶׁר צִוָּה יְהוָה אֶל־מֹשֶׁה וַיַּנִּיחֵהוּ אַהֲרֹן לִפְנֵי הָעֵדֻת לְמִשְׁמָרֶת
As the LORD had commanded Moses, Aaron placed it
inside the Pact, to be kept for all generations.

Exodus 16:34

There are some things in this passage that are not very clear. The first one is what this "pact" would be and what is it that Aharon set inside it to be kept.

לִפְנֵי הָעֵדֻת - *before the pact - means before the Ark of the Covenant.*
Rashbam, Exodus 16:34

According to Rashbam, this verse is speaking about the Ark of the Covenant, the Aron HaKodesh. In the previous verse, verse 33, we are told that what was placed inside the Ark was an Omer of the Manah. This is where we should focus our attention, on the spiritual representation that this Manah has, for according to this passage, this Manah should have been kept "for all generations".

*By verbal analogy, the term GENERATIONS of Exodus
16:34 is understood to have the same meaning as
the term GENERATIONS written in reference to the
holy anointing oil as seen in Exodus 30:31.*
Talmud of Babylon, Tractate of Yoma 52b

*Since the anointing oil recipe precedes all miracles, it is not
surprising that its preparation and use also involve miracles, for
it is the oil that turns a man into a king and a man into a priest.*
Talmud of Jerusalem, Tractate Horayot 11b

According to our sages, the manah placed in the Ark of the Covenant has a direct connection with the anointing oil. They also claim that this oil works the miracle of turning a common man into a king or a priest.

*And he has on his clothing and on his thigh a name
written, KING OF KINGS, AND LORD OF LORDS.*
Revelations 19:16

*So also Mashiach glorified not himself to be made a high
priest; but he that said to him, You are my Son, to day have
I begotten you. As he said also in another place, You are
a priest for ever after the order of Melekh Tzadik.*
Hebrews 5:5-6

Ok, we have a lot of information for a simple message. The

verse from Exodus talks about something that should be placed inside the ark for all generations, one verse before, we find out that this thing is the manah that felt from the heavens. Our sages then teach us that the spiritual representation of the manah is seen in the anointing oil, an oil that performs miracles by turning a common man into a king or a priest. With this in mind, we have two statements about Yeshua from the New testament, one saying that he is king and the second saying he is also a priest.

Well, Yeshua Ben Yosef, in life, was none of them, nor king nor priest, however, at the moment of his death, the coming of this darkness represented something spiritual that was taking place at that very moment, for at that very moment he became a priest, the anointing oil miracle was hidden in that darkness, for only by becoming a priest was he able to perform the sacrifice he performed. That same darkness, that was operating as the anointing oil, also performed the miracle to make him a king, that is, at that moment he became ready and worthy to come back as Mashiach Ben David, the King of kings.

E) FROM THE KING OF JUDAH TO ISRAEL, THE SALVATION (3034)

וְיֵהוּא מָצָא אֶת־אֲחֵי אֲחַזְיָהוּ מֶלֶךְ־יְהוּדָה וַיֹּאמֶר מִי אַתֶּם וַיֹּאמְרוּ
אֲחֵי אֲחַזְיָהוּ אֲנַחְנוּ וַנֵּרֶד לִשְׁלוֹם בְּנֵי־הַמֶּלֶךְ וּבְנֵי הַגְּבִירָה

Yehu came upon the kinsmen of King Ahaziah of Judah.
"Who are you?" he asked. They replied, "We are the kinsmen
of Ahaziah, and we have come to pay our respects to the
sons of the king and the sons of the queen mother."

II Kings 10:13

Very briefly, this verse is part of the account of the time when King Ahaziah of Judah sends men to King Yehu from the Kingdom of Israel to pay respect for the death of his children. I particularly understand this in two ways, the first as the direction taken by a king of Judah, namely, the King of kings,

Mashiach, that will come from Judah towards the people from the Kingdom of Israel, as written elsewhere:

וְאַתָּה בֵּית־לֶחֶם אֶפְרָתָה צָעִיר לִהְיוֹת בְּאַלְפֵי יְהוּדָה מִמְּךָ לִי
יֵצֵא לִהְיוֹת מוֹשֵׁל בְּיִשְׂרָאֵל וּמוֹצָאֹתָיו מִקֶּדֶם מִימֵי עוֹלָם

And you, O Beit Lehem of Ephrath, Least among the clans of Judah, From you one shall come forth To rule Israel for Me. One whose origin is from of old, From ancient times.

Micah 5:1

The second form I understand it, is as a prophecy that has not yet come to pass. It will be when the Jews approach the real Mashiach at the moment they recognize him as such. This also could be a meaning for the darkness, a darkness that will be removed from before their eyes.

F) THE ANGEL OF SALVATION (3034)

כֹּה | אָמַר יְהוָה אַל־תַּשִּׁאוּ נַפְשֹׁתֵיכֶם לֵאמֹר הָלֹךְ
יֵלְכוּ מֵעָלֵינוּ הַכַּשְׂדִּים כִּי־לֹא יֵלֵכוּ

Thus said the LORD: Do not delude yourselves into thinking, "The Chaldeans will go away from us." They will not.

Jeremiah 37:9

In a Pessach celebration there are various customs, symbolic foods, the removal of the Chametz from home, reunion, family, and most importantly, the reading of the *Haggadah Shel Pessach*.

The Haggadah, after the Torah, is perhaps the most printed and best-selling book in Judaism. In this book one finds what must be done during the Passover celebration, the prayers, the blessings, everything. There are some different versions of Haggadot and the difference between them is found precisely in the prayers. The Haggadot are age-old books, some dating from times before the common age, some from the time of Yeshua and some a few years later. The truth is that these books contain many mysteries and revelations about what is one of the central pillars of the Jewish faith, the Mashiach.

Since the prophecy in question deals with the death of Yeshua, which occurred on a Pessach, I believe it makes total sense to make at least one connection between the prophecy from Amos with this biblical appointed time. So, let's take a look at what one of the Haggadah can teach us.

In one of the oldest Haggadah ever written, the Nirtzah Haggadah, one of its prayers states the following:

> *And now, the angel of Israel comes, for Mashiach Ben Yosef is being slain* **י''ע** *by the angel of death.*
> Nirtzah Haggadah Shel Passover, Chad Gadya 9

These words are very deep and revealing. At the very beginning appears "and now", this "now" refers to the moment when this blessing is read, that is, in a Pessach, the same time as Yeshua's death, so, this "now" can also be understood as the moment Yeshua died. Then it speaks about an Angel of Israel who comes because the angel of death is killing Mashiach Ben Yosef.

Our sages say that the angel treated here as "the Angel of Israel" is the same angel who came to retrieve Moses' body, the same angel who was upon Pinchas, Elijah, John the Baptist, and though not revealed his name, is the same angel who will bring Mashiach Ben David. For this reason, this was the angel that came to get Mashiach Ben Yosef, not allowing the angel of death to take him. This is the meaning of this prayer.

But my intention with all of this is to link Yeshua's death with Mashiach Ben Yosef through his connection with this Angel of Israel, because, as seen above, the verse of Amos that prophesies events that occurred in his death has a spiritual association with the verse of Jeremiah 37:9 (above), which has no apparent connection to the subject at hand.

The secret is found in the first and last letters of each word that makes up this verse. By separating the former together with their values, we have the following:

כֹּה אָמַר יְהוָה אַל תַּשִּׁאוּ נַפְשֹׁתֵיכֶם לֵאמֹר הָלֹךְ יֵלְכוּ מֵעָלֵינוּ הַכַּשְׂדִּים כִּי לֹא יֵלֵכוּ

Jeremiah 37:9

כ20 + א1 + י10+א1+ת400 + נ50 + ל30 + ה5 +
י10 + מ40 + ה5 + כ20 + ל30 + י10
= **632**

632 is a mystical value related to Pinchas, Elias and Ben Yosef, for it is the value of the one who was with them:

MAL´AKH ISRAEL (מלאך ישראל) - ANGEL OF ISRAEL
מ40 + ל30 + א1 + ך20 + י10 + ש300 + ר200 + א1 + ל30
= **632**

The last letters of each word together with their numerical values also reveal another very significant value:

כֹּה אָמַר יְהוָה אַל תַּשִּׁאוּ נַפְשֹׁתֵיכֶם לֵאמֹר הָלֹךְ יֵלְכוּ מֵעָלֵינוּ הַכַּשְׂדִּים כִּי לֹא יֵלֵכוּ

Jeremiah 37:9

ה5 + ר2 + ה5 + ל30 + ו6 + ם40 + ר2 + ן2 + ו6 + ו6 + ם40 + י10 + א1 + ו6
= **8**

MASHIACH BEN YOSEF (משיח בן יוסף)
מ40 + ש3 + י10 + ח8 + ב2 + ן5 + י10 + ו6 + ס60 + ף8
= **8**

What Jeremiah is showing us is precisely what Haggadah Shel Passover talks about concerning the Angel of Israel who came during the death of Mashiach Ben Yosef on a Pessach. And this is not all, this Haggadah blessing has a very strange abbreviation in the middle of its prayer that has no translation, a term that I have left as it is and bolded, as seen above.

In Hebrew some abbreviations of terms or names are customary, such as HaKADOSH BARUCH HU (הקדוש ברוך הוא), which means THE HOLY ONE, BLESSED BE HE, is written (הב"ה) using only its first letters in the abbreviation. When a holy name appears, such as the tetragram for example (י-ה-ו-ה) it is customary to abbreviate the first letter along with the last letter, but in this case, they are inverted for dealing with something holy, that is, it is placed the last letter first and then the first letter after, in the case of the tetragram we would have (הי).

The abbreviation that appears in this Haggadah is (ע"י) which is the first and last letter of the name of Yeshua (ישוע) in inverted position, so much so that the name YESHUA also has a value 8, the same value as MASHIACH BEN YOSEF (above).

By this we understand that this prophecy about the death of Yeshua also reveals to us the angel who came for him, thus confirming his mission as Ben Yosef. Moreover, this confirms that he is also Mashiach Ben David, for it is this angel who, according to our sages, will pave the way for his coming. This is all known by the sages, a knowledge that will never be openly revealed by them.

DAY, HOUR AND 3000 YEARS
One thing catches my attention, why does Matthew report the hours when the world went dark? Why from the third (noon) until the ninth (3 p.m.)? Leaving aside what I proposed so far for a while, I would like to suggest a very interesting commentary:

> *Just as a biblical day represents a thousand years, so the biblical hour can be understood through such an interpretation.*
>
> Iggeret HaGra 7

According to rabbinic knowledge and interpretation, just as

one day represents a thousand years, so too can one hour be taken into account. If so, the three hours of darkness may represent 3000 years of darkness. But what could this darkness be?

> *Rabbi Eliezer says: just as the day is followed by darkness and then the light returns, so too, even if it becomes darkness for the lost tribes, God will definitely bring them out of darkness.*
> Talmud of Babylon, Tractate Sanhedrin 110b

According to Rabbi Eliezer, we can understand this darkness as the dispersion of the tribes of Israel. So, perhaps, these three hours of darkness could be 3000 years of dispersion of the tribes. If we understand that this darkness was born together with the idolatry in which these people became involved around the year 921 b.c.e. we will see that the 3000 years later would fall around the year 2079 of our era. Maybe, I repeat, maybe, this year could mean something.

We'll only know when the day comes.

VINEGAR

וַיִּתְּנוּ בְּבָרוּתִי רֹאשׁ וְלִצְמָאִי יַשְׁקוּנִי חֹמֶץ

They give me MARAH for food, vinegar to quench my thirst.
Psalm 69:22

*And they gave him wine mixed with MARAH (Extract
from an extremely bitter plant). But when he began
to drink, he noticed it and did not drink.*
Matthew 27:34

The Pharisees had a little-known costume well approached
by the Oral Torah. If there were a death sentence, it was a rabbinical commandment to alleviate the suffering of the con-
demned; the Talmud reports some mixtures that should have
been made in order to help the physical pain caused by the
punishment of death, such an attitude is related, in an unclear
manner, by the book of Matthew in the above passage. One of
these formulas is a mixture of wine with marah and it is used
as an anesthetic for pain. The person who tried to give this
mixtures to Yeshua was a Pharisee for certain who tried to
easy his pain, for this is what the Oral Torah determines.

Returning to the prophetic Psalm; this verse alone has more
information than many verses from the Tanakh altogether.
For this reason, I will separate it into two parts, part A dealing
with food and part B dealing with drink. Using these words
(marah and vinegar), some diverse topics will be addressed.

Part A

וַיִּתְּנוּ בְּבָרוּתִי רֹאשׁ

They give me MARAH for food...

The first thing that struck me about this verse is the word its author used to define something bitter, poisonous, which is the word ROSH (ראש). This word means head, leadership or leader in its most common usage, but here it comes with another connotation. The interpretation of this term as marah comes from rabbinic teachings:

ROSH (רֹאשׁ) here is marah.

Tehilim meRashi

This surprised me, as Rashi uses the same term that appears in the Gospel of Matthew in its original language, Hebrew. In it, the author states that the mixture given to Yeshua, translated as gall in English, is actually wine with marah, the same marah defined by the rabbis for the term ROSH (ראש) found in this passage in Psalms and this is something good to know, for it is a strong rabbinical confirmation between this Psalm and what is related by Matthew. We must understand one thing, the factual confirmation, where both facts happen equally, as prophecy is defined, is one thing and the Rabbinic confirmation is a different thing, this confirmation does not take place by comparing the events, but it is when the mysteries of a certain prophecy are fulfilled and understood.

The verse begins with the verb ITNU (יתנו), a future conjugation of the third person plural of the verb LATET (לתת) - *to give*. However, this same conjugated word, ITNU (יתנו), is also the future third-person conjugated form of the verb LEHATNOT (להתנות), which means "to condition" or "to stipulate".

The second term that appears is BEBARUTI (בברותי) and it can be divided in several ways, for within that word, there are many others.

בברותי

First is the letter BET (ב). When linked to other words it has the meaning of "by" or "in the" or "for".

בברותי

We also find the term BAR (בר), which in Aramaic means son.

בברותי

The name RUTH (רות) is also found here.

By gathering all the information I've presented so far, we can read this part A in a different way, as follows:

It was stipulated in the son of Ruth the leadership...
Psalm 69:22a - rereading

The Tanakh tells that Ruth was a Gentile woman who marries a man of the tribe of Yehudah, she then converts herself to the God of Israel and from her offspring King David came and, in turn, Mashiach. Then it is possible to interpret this "son" who was stipulated as leader as being David, because he became king. However, this Psalm was written by David while he was already king, thus making his words unfeasible to be a prophecy and by that, we understand that this son who the prophecy talks about can only be one person, Mashiach!

Part B

וְלִצְמָאִי יַשְׁקוּנִי חֹמֶץ
...vinegar to quench my thirst.

This part begins with the word LITZMAI (לצמאי), a word formed by four other terms, but the interesting thing is the numerical value this word has as it is presented to us:

LITZMAI (לצמאי) - MY THIRST
ל30 + צ90 + מ40 + א1 + י10
= **171**

That value, 171, reminded me of a place that has the same numerical value, a place mentioned in two biblical accounts:

PENIEL (פניאל)
30ל + 1א + 10י + 50נ + 80פ
= **171**

*So Jacob named the place **Peniel,** meaning, "I have seen a divine being face to face, yet my life has been preserved."*
Genesis 32:31

*Yeroboam fortified Shechem in the hill country of Ephraim and resided there; he moved out from there and fortified **Peniel.***
I Kings 12:25

Peniel is the junction of two words, PANIM (פנים) - *face* - and EL (אל) - *God*. It was the place where Yaakov wrestled with a divine being and had his name changed to Israel. Then this place comes back on the scene, but in this case, history tells us that it was a city that has been fortified by the king of the northern kingdom and became the capital of Israel, thus representing this kingdom; those two informations are good enough to make this prophecy from the book os Psalm fully coherent.

The second word from this part is YASHKUNI (ישקוני), from the verb LEHASHKOT (להשקות) - *to irrigate*.

YASHKUNI (ישקוני)
1י + 50נ + 6ו + 1ק + 3ש + 1י
= **8**

MASHIACH BEN YOSEF (משיח בן יוסף)
8ף + 60ס + 6ו + 1י + 50ן + 2ב + 8ח + 1י + 3ש + 4מ
= **8**

And lastly, the word vinegar:

CHOMETZ (חמץ) - VINEGAR
90ץ + 40מ + 8ח
= **138**

The same value of the word LAKAKH (לקח) - *he took, taken*.

LAKAKH (לקח) - HE TOOK / TAKEN
ל30 + ק100 + ח8
= **138**

Now, as with part A, a rereading is also possible according to what has been calculated by Gematria:

... And Peniel (Kingdom of Israel), by Mashiach
Ben Yosef, will be taken (rescued).

Psalm 69: 22b - rereading

What this verse reveals is the two facets of Mashiach, Ben David, presented as "son of Ruth" and destined to lead and his second facet, Ben Yosef, whose mission was to rescue the tribes of Israel from among the Gentiles.

Here we have something fantastic, because it is yet another proof that both Ben David and Ben Yosef will be two facets of the same person, two different missions of the same Mashiach and not two different messiahs as many believe. Mashiach is one, with missions given at different times in human history.

The Proof

But how to prove what has been seen so far? Interestingly, all this is confirmed directly and mystically in the last two verses of this same chapter:

כִּי אֱלֹהִ**ם ֫** יֹ֘ושִׁ֤יע צִיֹּ֗ון וְ**יִ֫בְ֫נֶה** עָרֵ֥י יְהוּדָ֑ה וְ**יָֽ֫שְׁבוּ** שָׁ֗ם וִירֵשֽׁוּהָ
לז וְזֶ֣רַע עֲ֭בָדָיו יִנְחָל֑וּהָ וְאֹהֲבֵ֥י שְׁ֝מֹ֗ו יִשְׁכְּנוּ־בָֽהּ
For God will deliver Tzion and rebuild the cities of Judah; they
shall live there and inherit it; the offspring of His servants shall
possess it; those who cherish His name shall dwell there.

Psalm 69:36-37

Verse 36, which speaks about Tzion, about Israel, has two messages. The first is who will delivery Tzion and the second, the name of that deliverer. From the first MEM (מ / ם) and from right to left with a count of 12 letters, we have the letter BET

(ב) and 12 other letters, the letter YUD (י), thus forming the initials of MASHIACH BEN YOSEF (משיח בן יוסף).

כִּי אֱלֹהִים **יוֹשִׁיעַ** צִיּוֹן וְיִבְנֶה עָרֵי יְהוּדָה וְיָשְׁבוּ שָׁם וִירֵשׁוּהָ

Psalm 69:36

This Psalm is strongly linked to Ben Yosef's facet, for it will be through him that Adonai will save the tribes.

The psalmist also reveals the name of this Mashiach Ben Yosef mentioned in this verse. The word translated as "deliver" (as highlighted above) - YOSHIA (יושיע) - has the root formed by the letters (י-ש-ע), such letters are also used to form the name YESHUA (ישוע). That is, the name of Mashiach Ben Yosef is Yeshua, in this case, YEHOSHUA (יהשוע).

Verse 37 presents us with the other side of this story, he does not talk about salvation, but about servants, that is, for there to be a servant, there must be a leader. BEN DAVID (בן דוד) facet has a numerical value of 3, based on this value and its multiples, you can analyze verse 37 in a very interesting way:

וְזֶרַע עֲבָ**דָ**יו יִנְחָלוּהָ וְאֹהֲ**בֵ**י שְׁ**מוֹ** יִשְׁכְּנוּ־בָהּ

Psalm 69:37

From left to right, the third (3x1) letter from the first MEM (מ) is the letter BET (ב), whereas the letter DALET (ד) is the twelfth (3x4) letter from the letter BET (ב). Thus we have (מ-ב-ד), which is the initial letters of the name MASHIACH BEN DAVID (משיח בן דוד).

Using exactly the same counting form, multiples of 3, verse 37 still reveals one more secret:

וְזֶ**רַע** עֲבָדָיו יִנְחָלוּהָ וְ**אֹ**וֹהֲבֵי שְׁ**מוֹ** **י**ִשְׁכְּנוּ־בָהּ

Psalm 69:37

Starting from the first YUD (י) and counting from left to right and multiplying 3, once again appears the name YESHUA (ישוע), but unlike the previous verse, this time this name is connected with Mashiach Ben David, that is, Yeshua is also the name of Mashiach Ben David, as well as the name of Mashiach Ben Yosef.

I now believe that we have sufficient evidence to understand the subject that this chapter os Psalms addresses and why it was used by Matthew on his account on Yeshua's death. Despite a rather indirect form and perhaps, unbeknownst to the New Testament writers, the marah given to Yeshua shortly before his death was not a fulfillment of a prophecy, but rather to serve as a message to all, the message that he is both BEN YOSEF and BEN DAVID, that his death will reunite ISRAEL through his teaching of TORAH and through his lifestyle (TORAH), those who follow him will be those who will inherit God's chosen lands and serve Mashiach there, Mashiach Ben David.

May it be in our days!

THE LIFESTYLE

There is no way to talk about Mashiach without talking about Torah and how it defined his lifestyle. As mentioned before, one of the missions of Mashiach Ben Yosef is to bring the correct interpretation of the Torah and how it should be understood and observed.

What few know, and this is because of the poor translations into Western languages, is that Yeshua, in the vast majority of his related teachings, did not preach the Torah itself, but they were debates concerning what the Jews call as the Oral Torah. This "second" Torah is a compilation of rabbinical teachings concerning how the Laws of the Torah should be observed; Throughout its volumes, known today as the Talmud and Gemarah, rabbis discuss and set rules that sometimes help and sometimes replace what God determines in His Torah, thus making the rabbinic commandments, in many cases, more important to Jews than The word of God itself.

For this reason Yeshua debated a great deal with Pharisees from schools other than his own, such as those who came from Rabbi Shammai's school, who had an extremely religious and Jewish interpretation of the Torah. With this we can understand this mission of Mashiach, since his interpretation went against the human interpretation, he made room to impose what he had as truth and to establish the true way of living the Torah.

Such a mission and such lifestyle certainly have been included in the prophecies and one that we can find such a feat is found precisely in this Psalm that deals with vinegar. David uses two key words in this verse, they are ROSH (ראש) - *marah* - and CHOMETZ (חמץ) - *vinegar*. Through these two words, Gematria reveals to us the lifestyle of Yeshua, as follows:

ROSH (ראש)

6ש + 1א + 2ר

= **6**

CHOMETZ (חמץ)

9ץ + 4מ + 8ח

= **21**

By Mispar Katan's calculation, ROSH (ראש) has a value of 6 and CHOMETZ (חמץ) a value of 21. If we add both, 6 plus 21, we get a total of 27 and 27 is the value of God-determined way of life and the lifestyle that Mashiach came to teach:

TORAH CHAII (תורה חיי)

1י + 1י+ 8ח + 5ה + 2ר + 6ו + 4ת

= **27**

The term TORAH CHAII (תורה חיי) can be translated as TORAH LIVES or TORAH LIFESTYLE. Thus we can see that the psalmist reveals the lifestyle of Mashiach, the lifestyle as determined by the Torah as well as he is the living Torah, as written by John in the first chapter of his gospel.

A COMPLEX PROPHECY

In short, we must understand that the reason for the marah and wine mixture have been reported wasn't simply to show how much he suffered, or to make a connection between his death story with prophetic words. The account of this fact was to prove not only that he came as Mashiach Ben Yosef and in Israel's rescue, but also to prove that he will also come as Mashiach Ben David, the leader, for both are just two facets of the same person.

This account also reveals to us the lifestyle he led, taught and propagated, the Torah! Without the Torah, he could never have declared himself Mashiach Ben Yosef. Without the Torah, he could never have been declared as Mashiach Ben David, for by the Torah commandments he will rule. The mystical connection between Yeshua and the Torah is extremely important, because without his interpretation about it, he could not be seen as Mashiach.

> *The facets of Mashiach are hidden in the face of the Torah (words of the Torah). It is upon the face of the Torah that the spirit of Mashiach hovers, just as the spirit of Elohim hovered over the face of the abyss (Gen. 1:2). This alludes to the spirit of Mashiach, for his spirit hovers over the Torah, which represents the water of life and his lifestyle.*
> Likutei Moharan, Part II, Torah 32:2

MASHIACH, THE PRIEST

וְשָׁפַכְתִּי עַל־בֵּית דָּוִיד וְעַל | יוֹשֵׁב יְרוּשָׁלַם רוּחַ חֵן וְתַחֲנוּנִים וְהִבִּיטוּ אֵלַי אֵת
אֲשֶׁר־דָּקָרוּ וְסָפְדוּ עָלָיו כְּמִסְפֵּד עַל־הַיָּחִיד וְהָמֵר עָלָיו כְּהָמֵר עַל־הַבְּכוֹר

And I will pour on the house of David, and on the inhabitants of Jerusalem, the spirit of grace and of supplications: and they shall look on me whom they have pierced, and they shall mourn for him, as one mourns for his only son, and shall be in bitterness for him, as one that is in bitterness for his firstborn.
Zechariah 12:10

כִּי סְבָבוּנִי כְּלָבִים עֲדַת מְרֵעִים הִקִּיפוּנִי כָּאֲרִי יָדַי וְרַגְלָי
יח אֲסַפֵּר כָּל־עַצְמוֹתָי הֵמָּה יַבִּיטוּ יִרְאוּ־בִי
יט יְחַלְּקוּ בְגָדַי לָהֶם וְעַל־לְבוּשִׁי יַפִּילוּ גוֹרָל

Dogs surround me; a pack of evil ones closes in on me, like lions [they maul] my hands and feet. I take the count of all my bones while they look on and gloat. They divide my clothes among themselves, casting lots for my garments.
Psalms 22:17-19

Whey they placed him in the beam they shared his garments by lot.
Matthew 27:35

This verse from Zechariah is a classic passage that deals about Mashiach Ben Yosef, all Jewish rabbinic teaching attests this. According to the Jewish mindset, Mashiach Ben Yosef could come in two ways, if the people were worthy, he would come in a glorious way and win the wars of the people of Israel, if the people were not worthy, he would come in a simple and almost imperceptible way, teaching only a few and in the end, he would be killed by the Gentiles.

> *I will pour grace and supplication upon Jerusalem before they pass through a hard time, for they have killed Mashiach Ben Yosef and provoked the wrath of God. But in the end, all the Gentiles will look to the Creator and see what He will do to them, for by them Mashiach was slain.*
>
> Ibn Ezra, Zechariah 12:10

> *God will bring a sentence upon those who killed Mashiach Ben Yosef.*
>
> Abarbanel, Zechariah 12:10

> *As many men despise their only begotten, we also despised Mashiach Ben Yosef and therefore, he was killed.*
>
> Rashi, Zechariah 12:10

In addition to these intriguing commentaries, an analysis using Gematria on this verse could be interesting. The sum of its letters has a total value of 6073, thus linking it with a passage from the book of Leviticus that has the same numerical value:

> וַיָּשֶׂם אֶת־הַמִּצְנֶפֶת עַל־רֹאשׁוֹ וַיָּשֶׂם עַל־הַמִּצְנֶפֶת אֶל־מוּל פָּנָיו
> אֵת צִיץ הַזָּהָב נֵזֶר הַקֹּדֶשׁ כַּאֲשֶׁר צִוָּה יְהוָה אֶת־מֹשֶׁה
> *And he set the headdress on his head; and on the headdress, in front, he put the gold crown, the holy crown, as the LORD had commanded Moses.*
>
> Leviticus 8:9

Although this passage does not have an obvious appearance with the what we have been seen so far, there is a commentary about it that may reveal something pretty amazing:

> *The garment made the Levite worthy to sacrifice for Israel; if he or the people are not worthy, he will be killed by the hands of God.*

Rashi, Leviticus 8:9

Look how interesting this passage in Leviticus is, it deals with the priestly garments (see above that what was distributed from Yeshua was precisely his garments), which made those who clothed them worthy to sacrifice for Israel. Rashi says that if a man wears them and is not worthy of them or if the people he represents are not worthy, he will be killed by the hands of God.

Now the main point; the rabbis claim that if the people are not worthy of Mashiach, when he comes as Mashiach Ben Yosef, he will surely be killed because due to the people unworthiness. With this in mind we are able to understand another prophecy related to one of the attributes associated with Yeshua, the priesthood. The fact that his garments were quoted in both the gospel and in the prophecies, shows us that he was also given priestly authority.

They clothed Yeshua with silk garments and covered him with a greenish silk robe. They made a crown of thorns and placed it on his head and set a reed in his right hand and were bowing down mocking him. Peace be upon you, king of the Jews.

Matthew 27:28-29

What happened to his garments were mentioned by the gospel because it was a secret message about an unknown authority that it was given to Yeshua by God, an authority that gave him the right, according to the Torah, to sacrifice.

THE CROWN OF
BEN YOSEF

וְשָׁפַכְתִּי עַל־בֵּית דָּוִד וְעַל יוֹשֵׁב יְרוּשָׁלֵַם רוּחַ חֵן וְתַחֲנוּנִים וְהִבִּיטוּ אֵלַי אֵת
אֲשֶׁר־דָּקָרוּ וְסָפְדוּ עָלָיו כְּמִסְפֵּד עַל־הַיָּחִיד וְהָמֵר עָלָיו כְּהָמֵר עַל־הַבְּכוֹר

*And I will pour on the house of David, and on the inhabitant
of Jerusalem, the spirit of grace and of supplications: and
they shall look on me whom they have pierced, and they shall
mourn for him, as one mourns for his only son, and shall be in
bitterness for him, as one that is in bitterness for his firstborn.*
Zechariah 12:10

כִּי סְבָבוּנִי כְּלָבִים עֲדַת מְרֵעִים הִקִּיפוּנִי כָּאֲרִי יָדַי וְרַגְלֵי

*For dogs have compassed me: the assembly of the wicked
have enclosed me: they pierced my hands and my feet.*
Psalms 22:17

*They made a crown of thorns and placed it on his head
and set a reed in his right hand and were bowing down
mocking him. Peace be upon you, king of the Jews.*
Matthew 27:29

This passage from the book of Zechariah is well known in the
Jewish milieu as a prophetic passage regarding the death of
Mashiach Ben Yosef. According to the rabbinic understanding, Ben Yosef would be killed by the hands of the Gentiles,
something that came to pass by the hands of the Romans;
then the prophet speaks about the annihilation that will be

brought upon the nations because they killed Mashiach since they did not recognize him, that is, not a recognition of knowing that he existed, but a recognition that deals with believing through the understanding in who he really is and not in a being that looks like him, as the christian jesus for example.

I will bring up two commentaries from two great sages about the prophecy above; the first one is from Ibn Ezra, who claims an absolute truth, as follows:

> *I will pour grace and supplication upon Jerusalem before*
> *they pass through a hard time, for they have killed Mashiach*
> *Ben Yosef and provoked the wrath of God. But in the end,*
> *all the Gentiles will look at the Creator and see what He*
> *will do to them, for by them Mashiach was slain.*
>
> Ibn Ezra, Zechariah 12:10

One thing is for sure, when Mashiach Ben David comes, he will crush all pagan beliefs and all those who falsely came in his name, or in the name of a false Mashiach. In the second commentary, Radak claims the same, and more, he states that Mashiach Ben Yosef is the savior of the Gentiles, but due to the Gentiles' lack of understanding, they did not recognize him:

> *Mashiach Ben Yosef, who will be the savior of the*
> *Gentiles, will not be understood by them. It intrigues*
> *me what they will say when the day comes.*
>
> Radak, Zechariah 12:10

Both commentaries are impressive and show a reality that is yet to come. Christianity aside, my purpose is to prove the Jewish consensus that this verse deals with Mashiach Ben Yosef; this is a further proof of why Yeshua had his feet and hands pierced when he was nailed to the tree, for it was a prophetic act that reveals the misunderstanding that took place about him in the gentile world.

Another thing we must take into account is why the verse, in its first words, states "the **inhabitant** of Jerusalem" in the singular form (differently from some western translations that are in the plural form)?

To answer that question, we just have to look at just these words in Hebrew:

וְשָׁפַכְתִּי עַל־בֵּית דָּוִיד וְעַל יוֹשֵׁב יְרוּשָׁלַם
And I will pour on the house of David, and on the inhabitant of Jerusalem...

Starting with the last letter and going from left to right, we have the MEM SOFIT (ם / מ) and by using multiples of 6, we will have as the sixth (6x1 = 6) letter the letter BET (ב) and as the twelfth (6x2 = 12) the letter YUD (') and this stands for:

MASHIACH (משיח - ם / מ)
BEN (בן - ב)
YOSEF (יוסף - ')

This answers my question and confirms who this "singular inhabitant" is; this is a prophecy directly linked to Ben Yosef and shows what that rabbis have been stating, he is the one who will be killed by the Gentiles. However, there is so much more in those prophecies than meets the eyes.

THE CROWN
This verse, when studied further, not only deals with Mashiach Ben Yosef, but it also deals with priesthood, something that, according to the New Testament writers, was also above Yeshua's head.

In order to deeply understand the prophecies, we must start with the full value of the verse of Zechariah 12:10, which is 6073. Throughout the Torah, there is a single passage with that same value, thus stablishing a connection between them.

וַיָּשֶׂם אֶת־**הַמִּצְנֶפֶת** עַל־רֹאשׁוֹ וַיָּשֶׂם עַל־**הַמִּצְנֶפֶת** אֶל־מוּל פָּנָיו
אֵת צִיץ הַזָּהָב נֵזֶר הַקֹּדֶשׁ כַּאֲשֶׁר צִוָּה יְהוָה אֶת־מֹשֶׁה

*And he set the **headdress** on his head; and on the*
***headdress**, in front, he put the gold crown, the holy*
crown, as the LORD had commanded Moses.

Leviticus 8:9

At first we have two completely disconnected verses; however, there is a small term that connects both passages, for during the death of Yeshua, something occurred alongside with what was described by Zechariah; before Yeshua was pierced, they placed on his head a HAMITZNEFET (המצנפת). The Hebrew word for crown is KETER (כתר), however, the word "mitznefet" used by the book of Leviticus, means anything that could be placed above one's head, a headdress, such as a cap, a bonnet, a turban or even a crown of thorns. From this we can begin to see the strange connection that both verses have, even if their main topics have nothing to do with one another.

But the question is, was Yeshua crowned only as a mockery for he declared himself to be the king of the Jews, or is there something spiritually deeper behind this fact?

Holiness's accessories, the ark, the golden breastplate and
the mitznefet (crown). Whoever used them possessed
the holiness of the Torah above their lives.

Rashi, Numbers 31:6

According to Rashi, all those who wore the headdress or the breastplate or anything holy, had the holiness of the Torah above their lives. By this we can understand that Yeshua's crown spiritually represented the holiness of Yeshua and such a holiness that is directly connected to the Torah.

What many do not understand is that Yeshua lived, preached, and never abolished anything from the Torah. As a Pharisee rabbi, servant of the living God of Israel, he could in no way have a life outside the Torah standards, let alone propagate a life without it in the way many Christians believe and teach. Let's see some passages in this regard, translated from its original language:

> *Yeshua answered and said to him, permit it, because we are obliged to fulfill all that makes one a tzadik (one who observes the Torah), them Yohanan submersed him.*
>
> Matthew 3:15

> *Ashrei will be you when you are persecuted and rebuked and when they tell you many bad things because the Torah, all falsely spoken.*
>
> Matthew 5:11

> *At that time Yeshua said to his talmidim: do not think that I came to violate the Torah, but to observe it in its completeness. Truly, I say to you that even if the heavens and the earth (depart), a yud or a nekudah will not be abolished from the Torah or the prophets and everything will be fulfilled. And whoever fails to perform some Torah Mitzvot, however small it is and teaches it to others to do so, will be called HAVEL (futile) in the Kingdom of Heaven and whoever observes and teaches Mitzvot of the Torah, great will be called in the Kingdom of Heaven.*
>
> Matthew 5:17-19

> *Because not everyone who says unto me, lord, will enter the kingdom of heaven, but the one who does the Torah of my father who is in heaven will enter the kingdom of heaven.*
>
> Matthew 7:21

> *Take my yoke as your yoke and learn from my Torah, for I am humble, I am good and pure in heart and you will find rest in your souls.*
>
> Matthew 11:29

> *The son of man will send his angels to uproot from his kingdom all evil and all who does not follow the Law (TORAH).*

Matthew 13:41

Other than that, besides living the Torah, one of his missions was to interpret it, otherwise he could never have been called Mashiach Ben Yosef, for the holiness that was above his life shows that he had the correct interpretation of Torah and this is one of the reason that the headdress, or the crown, was placed above his head, for it was saying that he was holy due to the Torah and for this reason, everything he taught about it, is the correct interpretation and must be followed, that was his real kingship as Ben Yosef.

One last thing to bear in mind is to whom, according to the Torah, this headdress, this mitznefet, is intended. Now, both the breastplate and the headdress were holy objects that the priest should wear during any sacrifice; Yeshua's crown also represented the priesthood of Ben Yosef, for at the time he became a sacrifice he had to wear the holy object as stipulated by the Torah, for Yeshua lived it until his last breath, thus showing his liaison with the Torah and the holy priesthood. A proof of this is found in the word HAMITZNEFET itself:

HAMITZNEFET (המצנפת)
ה5 + מ4 + צ9 + נ5 + פ8 + ת4
= **8**

MASHIACH BEN YOSEF (משיח בן יוסף)
מ4 + ש3 + י1 + ח8 + ב2 + נ5 + י1 + ו6 + ס6 + ף8
= **8**

HACOHEN (הכהן) - THE PRIEST
ה5 + כ2 + ה5 + ן5
= **8**

He was crowned not as king, but as Ben Yosef the priest and as one who holds the true knowledge about the Torah. I believe that through this understanding the author of Hebrews writes the following:

Now of the things which we have spoken this is the sum: We have such an high priest, who is set on the right hand of the throne of the Majesty in the heavens; A minister of the sanctuary, and of the true tabernacle, which the Lord pitched, and not man. For every high priest is ordained to offer gifts and sacrifices: why it is of necessity that this man have somewhat also to offer.

Hebrews 8:1-3

Well, if his death as Mashiach served to bring salvation, that is, the Torah, to the world, what did his death as a priest represent? A very interesting passage from the Talmud answers this question:

Gemarah asks: According to someone who said this is a mourning for the death of Mashiach Ben Yosef who was killed, the passage states "and they shall look on me whom they have pierced, and they shall mourn for him, as one mourns for his only son, and shall be in bitterness for him, as one that is in bitterness for his firstborn." (Zech 12:10) But what is the virtue in all this? It represents the death of Yetzer Harah (man's evil inclination).

Talmud of Babylon, Tractate Sukkah 52a

Yetzer Harah, or the evil inclination, is the antithesis of Yetzer Hatov, the good inclination. Every human being has both of them within and it is the obligation of each one not to be taken by the evil one. When the Talmud claims that the virtue of the death of Mashiach Ben Yosef is the death of the evil inclination, it does not claim that it ceased to exist, but it teaches that the man who lives his Torah will never be taken by the Yetzer Harah, so, Yeshua's Torah defeats the evil within.

Now, in order to bring all the informations together, let's first read a simple verse written by Peter:

Who his own self bore our sins in his own body on the tree, that we, being dead to sins, should live to righteousness: by whose stripes you were healed.

I Peter 2:24

Well, what many does not correctly understand about the death of Yeshua, is that he did not die to magically take away our sins, rather in fact, he died to bring the Torah to the Gentile world and through it and his interpretation on it, everyone could overcome the inner evil inclination by living a life without sins; this is the real interpretation of "taking away the sins", it is not a magical thing; to take away the sins is the opportunity given by God, through Yeshua's death, for every men to get to know what sin is and to live a life without it.

So we learn here that Ben Yosef's death as a priest is the opportunity given by God to every single soul to know sin and to get rid of it; this was the real meaning of his death as a priest, thus fulfilling his third mission, which is to remove the unclean spirit from the world, something only possible with the word of God and, as everyone knows, is at the hand of whoever wants to learn from it.

We also see here that this crown placed upon his head was to testify Yeshua's holiness due to his life according to the Torah, a holiness that made him worthy to be a sacrifice, it also confirms his priesthood, for this crown, in this case, was as a symbol for the priest's headdress, a headdress that made him spiritually capable to present a sacrifice before God and lastly, it shows the removal of the sin from the world, that is, it represents the opportunity given to everyone to have a life according to God's will.

AMEN

יְחַלְּקוּ בְגָדַי לָהֶם וְעַל־לְבוּשִׁי יַפִּילוּ גוֹרָל

*They divide my clothes among themselves, casting
lots for my garments.*

Psalms 22:19

Whey they placed him in the beam they shared his garments by lot.
Matthew 27:35

The word amen is undoubtedly the most recited word in all
of human history. Intriguing is the power this word has and
the influence it has on the three most important beliefs in the
world, Judaism, Christianity, and Islam. The earliest account
of Amen's history, that is, the first time it appears in docu-
mented history, is found in a Torah passage:

וּבָאוּ הַמַּיִם הַמְאָרֲרִים הָאֵלֶּה בְּמֵעַיִךְ לַצְבּוֹת בֶּטֶן
וְלַנְפִּל יָרֵךְ וְאָמְרָה הָאִשָּׁה אָמֵן | אָמֵן
*May this water that induces the spell enter your body,
causing the belly to distend and the thigh to sag."
And the woman shall say, "Amen, amen!"*

Numbers 5:22

The book Zohar HaKadosh says that those who utter the
amen after hearing a prayer or blessing are higher than those
who recite it.

*He who answers amen is greater and more valuable than he
who recites the blessing. Anyone who hears a blessing and does
not meditate on his heart in the amen, closes the gates and no*

blessing will be opened to him. Shame on him, shame on his soul.
Zohar V 22 7:36

Our sages say that those who understand the true secret meaning behind the word Amen will be blessed, guarded, saved, and protected from their enemies. Based on what our sages teach us, I ask, how can a single word have the power to close the heavenly gates and to prevent anyone from being truly blessed?

The literal meaning of the amen is well known: "so be it!" But that is certainly not why this word is so powerful. Understanding the amen just as a statement that will make the blessing or the recited prayer to come true is like eating only the peel of a fruit, only the outside, the superficial part, leaving all the flavor, vitamin and sustenance behind.

There is no way to understand this word before some simple, but difficult to understand at first glance, concepts are clarified. The Zohar sages teach us that there are ten emanations of God, such as the goodness, the grace, the mercy, the wisdom, the judgment and so on. Each of these emanations represents spiritual dimensions. These dimensions are where blessings, God's will, knowledge, wisdom, among others, are found. When these emanations reach the earthly reality, the will of the Creator becomes physical and the life of man is transformed, both for good or evil, in the case if God decides to bring a treatment upon one's life.

These emanations, that is, these dimensions represent 99% of all that God created in the spiritual realms and only 1% of what God created represents human reality, that is, everything we live and have as truth as human beings is only 1% of all that God generated and created. The Zohar also teaches us that this reality only exists because these emanations support it, for without them, it would be as if God has turned his back and left; it would be as if His influence and power simply ceased to exist. God forbid!

With this we can begin to understand the power of the amen, this simple word has the power to bring all these spiritual emanations into our reality, to make them tangible, and with that, God's will and plan in our lives will become real and unquestionable. The amen is like the power cord that connects the earthly world with the power outlet found in the spirit realm.

As we look at the Torah, we will see that God has 72 different names. In order to understand what has been seen so far, we must look at some things about two of them, the unpronounceable name of God (י-ה-ו-ה), as well as another name that appears a lot throughout the Tanakh, ADONAI (אדני).

The Zohar teaches that these emanations, which represent 99% of all God-created reality, are connected to the Tetragram (י-ה-ו-ה) and that is why God did not allow this name to be taken in vain, for it represents something that is above our physical reality, our understanding. On the other hand, the name ADONAI (אדני), which is also formed by four letters, represents the 1% of our physical reality and what man can achieve by his own understanding, because it is the simplest name of God. Now let's look at some numbers:

$$YWHW\ (\text{י-ה-ו-ה})$$
$$5\text{ה} + 6\text{ו} + 5\text{ה} + 10\text{י}$$
$$= \mathbf{26}$$

$$ADONAI\ (\text{אדני})$$
$$10\text{י} + 50\text{נ} + 4\text{ד} + 1\text{א}$$
$$= \mathbf{65}$$

If we put both names together, we get 26 + 65 = 91 and so it starts to make some sense, because:

$$AMEN\ (\text{אמן})$$
$$50\text{ן} + 40\text{מ} + 1\text{א}$$

= **91**

What we see here is that the word amen represents the connection of these two deep names of God. One representing the spiritual realm, the will of God and the other one representing the knowledge that human capabilities can achieve about who God is in this earthly reality; when both names are connected is as if a bridge were erected between the earthly and the spiritual reality. It is as if the power button were turned on in the spirit world and all its energy is felt here in this reality, in the life of man.

Every time a prayer or blessing does not materialize, it is because this energy, this "cable" that connects these two realities, is disconnected. This is why James states:

> *You ask, and receive not, because you ask amiss,*
> *that you may consume it on your lusts.*
>
> James 4:3

When man prays only for his own benefit, he clearly does not understand the true meaning of the amen, so his prayers will always be unconnected and many will never be answered. James, knowing about this concept, states that he who asks for himself alone doesn't know how to ask, because the man who asks for his own delight is one who is totally connected and dependent on material things, things that certainly blind him from understanding the true spiritual world, thus making him increasingly distant from a connection with God and the real purpose of the amen. The apostle's words make complete sense here.

Once again, the understanding of the amen is what manifests God's will in this reality, as well as all His manifestations, such as His goodness, mercy, wisdom, grace and so on.

Now we can return to the verse of the Psalms in question. Sure, like all the others seen in this book, this verse relates an historically accurate thing that happened to Yeshua, for before his death, he was stripped naked and his garments were distributed among the Roman soldiers. But the question is, what is the real reason for this statement? Why it have been reported? Or better, what is the real reason why this apparently insignificant fact was given as a prophecy? What is the truth behind this seemingly irrelevant event?

Well, if we look at this verse in Hebrew and use the first letters of each single word of this verse, with a bit of Gematria, we have the following:

$$\text{יְחַלְּקוּ בְגָדַי לָהֶם וְעַל לְבוּשִׁי יַפִּילוּ גוֹרָל}$$

$$\text{ג}3 + \text{י}10 + \text{ל}30 + \text{ו}6 + \text{ל}30 + \text{ב}2 + \text{י}10$$

$$= 91$$

What we see here is that the word Amen (91) is hidden in this verse, that is, this verse has a message. As the Amen is the will of God that comes from the spiritual world materializing in this reality, this psalm and the event of the casting lot of the garments of Yeshua, which I dare to call as a "prophetic act", represent a hidden message that is saying that in that very moment, the will of God in the spiritual realms had just materialized in Yeshua's life and in this earthly reality.

To make it clear what God's will was, I will bring up two passages from some rabbis who understood much of what is being treated here:

> *He that spared not his own Son, but delivered him up for us all, how shall he not with him also freely give us all things?*
> Romans 8:32

> *For God so loved the world, that he gave his only begotten Son, that whoever believes in him should not perish, but have everlasting life.*
> John 3:16

Now we see what was God's will, the sacrifice of Yeshua. It was not due to the Roman, nor due to the judgment of the Jews, but what really killed Yeshua and made him as a sacrifice was the will of God Himself, a will that materialized in this realm at the moment that his garments were casted, and this same moment is when the rescue of Israel effectively began, for this is God's will and promise. So, we see here that this fact was only reported to show the significance of God's will to deliver his son in order to save His people Israel. All of this is proved by Yeshua's own words.

> *Then he said to them, my soul is grieved unto death, support me and watch with me. Then he went forward very slowly and fell on his face and prayed and said: if it is possible, may this cup be removed from me, please. But in fact, it may not be as I want it to be, but according to **Your will**.*
> Matthew 26:38-39

The casting of Yeshua's garments was the moment of the amen, the moment when what God planned came into our world and became reality, that is, the redemptive work of Mashiach Ben David, a work that needed the death of Ben Yosef to become possible, a death that was only possible by the connection between the spiritual realm and the earthly realm, thus reaching the 100% (99% + 1%) of God's will and plan. And all of this was for the mercy of us all.

As our sages teach:
AMEN (אמן): Amen has three letters: ALEF (א) MEM (מ) NUM (ן)
ALEF (אלף): DEEP WELL WHERE ALL BLESSINGS COME FROM. If you read it backwards, you read it as PELE (פלא) - miracle and wonder.
MEM (מ): River that runs on and on
NUN (נ): It is the matron who receives the blessings. Nun (ן) receives from Alef and Mem.

The word AMEN (אמן) is a bundle of energy, from which you receive the blessing. Each time we say AMEN at the end of a prayer, it is as if we have recited it. This word begets angels (MAL' AKH = 91) to come to us at the time of our death, just as it did with Yeshua as seen in another chapter.

THOSE WHO WERE CALLED

לָכֵן אֲחַלֶּק־לוֹ בָרַבִּים וְאֶת־עֲצוּמִים יְחַלֵּק שָׁלָל תַּחַת אֲשֶׁר הֶעֱרָה לַמָּוֶת
נַפְשׁוֹ וְאֶת־פֹּשְׁעִים נִמְנָה וְהוּא חֵטְא־רַבִּים נָשָׂא וְלַפֹּשְׁעִים יַפְגִּיעַ

*Assuredly, I will give him the many as his portion, He shall receive
the multitude as his spoil. For he exposed himself to death and
was numbered among the sinners, Whereas he carried the SIN
(singular form) of* **the many** *and made intercession for the* **rebels**.
Isaiah 53:12

*Then two thieves were hung with him, one
on his right and one on his left.*
Matthew 27:38

This is a widely known verse in the Christian milieu, it is used as one of many proofs of Yeshua's Messianism; something plausible, since it is taught that his death brought forgiveness of sins and that he interceded for sinners.

In the above translation, I tried to use a more directly translated words, which brings a slight difference from the versions that exist in Western languages, especially in the parts that appears that he carried the sin and his intercession was for the rebels. .

With this in mind, let's look at the term that appears in its original Hebrew as "rebels". By definition, a rebel is one who does not obey orders, that is, someone who is a part of a group that receives directives from superiors and, unlike the rest, he insists on not accepting the ordained and voluntarily acts contrary. The definition of the word leads us to understand that the "rebels", who received this intercession, were necessarily part of a group that received orders that defined sin, that is, the Torah. So we understand that this "rebels" are the people who were part of the twelve tribes of Israel and this term "rebels" is definitely not dealing with Gentiles or churches, as those did not have a relationship with God to rebel against.

As already seen about the tribes of Israel, the northern Torah-aware tribes were scattered and assimilated into pagan cultures. This was due to attitudes which, in God's eyes, were an affront, for despite all the knowledge they had obtained in all their years of existence, the people of the Kingdom of Israel rebelled against the word of the Creator and therefore, these rebels needed one who interceded for them.

This makes a strong connection with Yeshua's mission and work. Many understand that his death begot forgiveness of all sins as magic, but in fact it was not so; his death brought to all nations what defines sin and what teaches man to live a life without sins, the Word of God, in other words, his death gave the opportunity for all men to know the one true God, His will and purposes, and through this, man will have his sins forgiven; Not through magic, but through understanding that causes a change of life and behavior, then yes, the sins will be taken away thanks to the death of Yeshua.

Again, this brings us to Yeshua's own words:

> *And Yeshua said to them, I was not sent except to*
> *the lost sheep of the house of Israel.*
>
> Matthew 15:24

Today, the descendants of these tribes are scattered among the Gentiles, they will be gathered together again under the wings of God so that they may serve Mashiach, for this reason the word of God was taken to all nations through the sacrifice of Yeshua. When the time comes, in various parts of the world, among various creeds, an awakening to the Torah will occur with many people, thus separating the chaff from the wheat, the pagan from the saint, Israel from the Gentiles.

May it be in our days!

THE CALLED ONES

Another thing that we should pay attention to in this verse is the verb used as "carried" in Hebrew. The first thing to keep in mind, something that denies the Christian theological interpretation of this verse, is that the death of Yeshua carried the sin of MANY and not the sin of EVERYONE, that is, if sin were totally removed from this world, as many Christians teach, or that his death was for the benefit for all nations and creeds, then the verse would have said that he carried the sins of EVERYONE and not of MANY, and this shows that part of his mission was really directed to a particular group, treated by the prophet as "many" and as "rebels".

The Hebrew word for "carried" is NASSAH (נשא), from the verb LASSE'ET (לשאת) - *to carry*. With a Gematria analysis of this verb as it appears, we shall have:

NASSAH (נשא) - CARRIED
1א + 300ש + 50נ
= **351**

Another word that has the same value is NIKRAH (נקרא), which means CALLED or LINKED.

NIKRAH (נקרא)
1א + 200ר + 100ק + 50נ
= **351**

Now we can understand who are those who had the sin carried. In the Tanakh, this verb appears only once directly connected to a group of people:

כֹּל הַ**נִּקְרָא** בִשְׁמִי וְלִכְבוֹדִי בְּרָאתִיו יְצַרְתִּיו אַף־עֲשִׂיתִיו

All who are linked (NIKRAH) to My name, Whom I
have created, Formed, and made for My glory.

Isaiah 43:7

Now we have a definition for those "many" who had the sin carried; They are those who are connected to the name of the Creator, those who were created, formed and made for His glory. However, that still doesn't have a very precise definition, so, let's take a look at the previous verse:

I will say to the North (kingdom of Israel), "Give back!" And
to the South (kingdom of Judah), "Do not withhold! Bring My
sons from afar, And My daughters from the end of the earth.

Isaiah 43:6

What is the meaning of "Bring my sons from afar?" Rav
Huna says: it is the Diaspora Jews who are calm as sons
and therefore able to keep up with the study of the Torah.
And what is the meaning of "my daughters from the ends
of the Earth"? This represents Israel's lost tribes among
other nations, whose minds are restless, like daughters.

Talmud of Babylon, Tractate Menachot 110a

Now it is clear, the "many" who had the sin taken are the descendants of the tribes of Israel scattered throughout the nations, who, for being far from the Torah, are considered sinners and very well represented by the two thieves who were hanging by Yeshua's side, for they were also part of the people, but they got lost on the way. It is for these people that Yeshua died and it is for them that he interceded, it will be they who will be reunited with the Jewish people so that all may serve Mashiach.

The point is, nobody knows who the descendants of these tribes are, it could be you, me, our neighbor, the guy from the office, all of us, none of us, we don't know for sure; but the truth is that all of those who have a vocation to serve God out of love, and not out of bargain, through a sudden and unexplained awakening, certainly have the spark given to the whole nation of Israel at the foot of Mount Sinai, thus proving him to be a member of one of those lost tribes.

Another point to bear in mind in Isaiah's prophecy is something that goes against what is taught by Christian theology, which claims that Jesus died to take away all sins. According to Isaiah, Mashiach would die to bear the sin, not sinS.

As already discussed, the purification that God had to bring to Israel was referring to the sin of idolatry, it was by this sin that they were scattered, and it was due to this sin that God brought the living sacrifice to them. This can be confirmed by the verse connected to the above one from Isaiah. Its total value is 6601 and throughout the entire tanakh, only one verse has this same value, a verse found in the book of Ezekiel:

וַיַּמְרוּ־בִי וְלֹא אָבוּ לִשְׁמֹעַ אֵלַי אִישׁ אֶת־שִׁקּוּצֵי עֵינֵיהֶם לֹא
הִשְׁלִיכוּ וְאֶת־גִּלּוּלֵי מִצְרַיִם לֹא עָזָבוּ וָאֹמַר לִשְׁפֹּךְ חֲמָתִי
עֲלֵיהֶם לְכַלּוֹת אַפִּי בָּהֶם בְּתוֹךְ אֶרֶץ מִצְרָיִם

But they defied Me and refused to listen to Me. They did not cast away the detestable things they were drawn to, nor did they give up the fetishes of Egypt. Then I resolved to pour out My fury upon them, to vent all My anger upon them there, in the land of Egypt.
Ezekiel 20:8

Fantastic! Ezekiel in this verse talks about God's wrath and its motives. First he cites the "detestable things" that are the objects of idolatry and then the "fetish of Egypt" that is related to prostitution. According to the Tanakh, pagan practice is considered a prostitution, as it is if one cheats on God.

Thus we have the confirmation that the rebels are the descendants of the Kingdom of Israel, for the sin that Yeshua carried in his death was the sin of idolatry that was upon this people mentioned by Ezekiel, because it was due to idolatry that the people were scattered and, idolatry, as taught by the Torah, is a sin (curse) that passes on from generation to generation.

By the death of Yeshua and his intercession, this hereditary curse was broken so that these lost people may be clean once again to return to God's ways and to accept His Torah, to have a clean mind and heart to understand and to receive Him; thus fulfilling, again, two missions of Ben Yosef and paving the way for Ben David.

AUTHORITY

וַאֲנִי | הָיִיתִי חֶרְפָּה לָהֶם יִרְאוּנִי יְנִיעוּן רֹאשָׁם

*I am the object of their scorn; when they
see me, they shake their head.*

Psalm 109:25

Those who were passing by mocked him and shook heads.

Matthew 27:39

It makes me very curious how certain facts about Yeshua's life, facts that to some extent one may define as "irrelevant", have been reported in a way that perfectly match with some of David's Psalms. It is very difficult to say whether this was purposeful by the Gospel writers or even if David wrote them in a prophetic way. Whether they knew it or not, the fact is that much of what happened in the life of King David also took place in the life of Yeshua, and the most intriguing thing is that those facts are just ordinary facts, small things, things that many of those who study the New Testament only use them to associate the New Testament with the Tanakh

Among many cases, we have the above verse, where David claims he was mocked and that the people who saw him shook their heads in disapproval; then comes Matthew and reports the exact same terms in his account of Yeshua's death. But the most amazing thing is that it is in these small details, in these irrelevant events, that we find the greatest prophecies and revelations about God's plan and who really Mashiach is.

When one reproaches another, one can demonstrate such disapproval in some ways, such as through words, by both criticism and derision, as well as with a simple shake of one's head or by a look of disapproval. The fact is, a reprobation from someone only occurs in two cases, when the person clearly acts badly towards others or when the one who criticizes does not understand the reasons that led to the one who is being disapproved of taking such acts. In these two verses we are dealing with two people, David, a king and Yeshua, the Mashiach, which makes it clear that the reproach that came from these people fits the second case, there was something in the lives of both that those who shook their heads did not understand.

By Gematria, the verse 25 of chapter 109 of the book of Psalms has a total value of 1884. On top of this value we can find two other Torah passages that have exactly the same total value of 1884. The most striking is that the first passage reveals what would be what people did not understand and the second proves what the first revealed. God's word is impressive.

The first case is found in the first book of Samuel:

וַיֹּסֶף יְהוָה לְהֵרָאֹה בְ**שִׁלֹה** כִּי־נִגְלָה יְהוָה אֶל־שְׁמוּאֵל בְּ**שִׁלוֹ** בִּדְבַר יְהוָה

And the LORD continued to appear at SHILOH: the LORD revealed Himself to Samuel at SHILOH with the word of the LORD.

I Samuel 3:21

Clearly this passage has nothing to do with what happened to Yeshua and David, but it has an interesting term that repeats itself, one in which the verse revolves around. The word SHILOH (שילו), which is the name of an ancient city in the Samaria region. This name sometimes appears in the Tanakh, but oddly enough, almost never dealing with a city, but rather it normally deals with difficult to understand subjects.

The first case occurs in the book of Genesis. When Yaakov blesses his son Yehudah, he utters the following words:

לֹא־יָסוּר שֵׁבֶט מֵיהוּדָה וּמְחֹקֵק מִבֵּין רַגְלָיו עַד כִּי־יָבֹא
שִׁילֹה[שִׁילוֹ] וְלוֹ יִקְּהַת עַמִּים

*The scepter shall not depart from Judah, Nor the ruler's
staff from between his feet; until SHILOH shall come
to him and the homage of peoples be his.*

Genesis 49:10

Now, in that case, SHILOH is not a place, but something, or someone, that will come; and around that Shiloh all the people will come together. Here we have the first two things to be taken into account, SHILOH is someone and someone who is linked to Yehudah, to the tribe of Judah.

There is a very old Midrashic explanation of this term. Our sages define the Hebrew word SHILOH (שילו) as being the same as (לו שי) - *tribute to him* - as we can see in the book of Psalms:

נִדְרוּ וְשַׁלְּמוּ לַיהוָה אֱלֹהֵיכֶם כָּל־סְבִיבָיו יוֹבִי **לוּ שַׁי** לַמּוֹרָא

*Make vows and pay them to the LORD your God; -all who are
around Him shall bring tribute (שי) to the (לו) Awesome One.*

Psalms 76:12

Yaakov, in a mysterious way, already knew about Mashiach as seen in this Genesis passage quoted above, not only he knew about him, but also he revealed where this Shiloh would come from during the blessing to his son, Yehudah. The moment he casts the blessing, he speaks of the coming of a certain Shiloh and that the peoples will be gathered around. In the other hand, in the book of Psalms, we have the same term referring to someone, but in this case, as someone to whom everyone should bring tributes, someone Awesome.

If we connect them both, I may ask, who will come from

the tribe of Judah, to whom all will bring tributes, to whom everyone will gather around and is also awesome? Easy one, MASHIACH! However, we must be a little careful here, for SHILOH is not simply Mashiach, for this a term that refers to something specific about Mashiach, something that David also possessed, and it is precisely this "something specific" that the mockers did not understand. Shiloh is actually what makes Mashiach worthy to receive tribute and to be feared by all. This something, the shiloh, is the AUTHORITY, for it is that what makes someone to be feared and worthy of receiving tributes.

Before any conclusions, we must know what this authority would be, above who it is and where it comes from. To this end, the second verse with the sum equal to 1884 comes in hand; it is found in the book of Jeremiah:

וְעָבְדוּ אֶת יְהוָה אֱלֹהֵיהֶם וְאֵת דָּוִד מַלְכָּם אֲשֶׁר אָקִים לָהֶם
Instead, they shall serve the LORD their God and
David, the king whom I will raise up for them.

Jeremiah 30:9

These words of Jeremiah have something very strange. He states that David will be raised as king, but how can this be possible, since David passed away 300 years before Jeremiah? That is, David had already been raised as king by that time.

The Holy One, Blessed Be He, is not dealing about King David in
Jr. 30:9, but about a new David for the Jewish people, Mashiach
Ben David, this is the reason that the prophecy is in the future.

Talmud of Babylon, Tractate Sanhedrin 98b

Now yes, this David that will be raised is not King David, but King Mashiach Ben David, and that reveals to us on whose shoulders will be the authority, around whom all peoples will be gathered, and to whom all will bring tribute, Mashiach Ben David, the form of Mashiach that was not recognized by the mockers, for Yeshua did not reign at that time.

Jeremiah further states that those who will come to Mashiach will not serve Mashiach, but will serve Adonai through Mashiach, through what he will establish as serving God should be. But what would that be?

There is an orthodox term which is DEREKH HATORAH (דרך התורה), which means the path stipulated by the Torah, a path that defines a lifestyle according to God's will, the value of this widely used expression is 3:

DEREKH HATORAH (דרך התורה) - WAY OF THE TORAH
ד4 + ר2 + ך2 + ה5 + ת4 + ו6 + ר2 + ה5
= **3**

If we do the same with the first 4 terms of Jeremiah's verse *"they shall serve the LORD their God"* it will be clear what this "serving Adonai" would be:

וְעָבְד֞וּ אֵת יְהוָה אֱלֹהֵיהֶם וְאֵת֙ דָּוִ֣ד מַלְכָּ֔ם אֲשֶׁ֥ר אָקִ֖ים לָהֶֽם
they shall serve the LORD their God....

Jeremiah 30:9

VeAVDU ET ADONAI ELOHEIHEM (ועבדו את יהוה אלהיהם)
- THEY SHALL SERVE THE LORD THEIR GOD
ו6 + ע7 + ב2 + ד4 + ו6 + א1 + ת4 + י1 + ה5 + ו6
+ ה5 + א1 + ל3 + ה5 + י1 + ה5 + מ5
= **3**

The Torah Way is the only way to serve the God of Israel. And finally, we will use the last words of the same verse:

וְעָבְד֞וּ אֵת יְהוָה אֱלֹהֵיהֶם וְאֵת֙ דָּוִ֣ד מַלְכָּ֔ם אֲשֶׁ֥ר אָקִ֖ים לָהֶֽם
....I will raise up for them

Jeremiah 30:9

AKIM LAKHEM (אקים להם) - I WILL RAISE UP FOR THEM
א1 + ק1 + י1 + מ4 + ל3 + ה5 + מ4

$$19 = 1+9 = \mathbf{10}$$

MASHIACH BEN DAVID (משיח בן דוד)

$$4ד + 6ו + 4ד + 5ן + 2ב + 8ח + 1י + 3ש + 4מ$$
$$= \mathbf{10}$$

Now it is clear as crystal. Adonai will raise up Mashiach Ben David so that through him and through his authority, which is the Torah, the Torah lifestyle will be established for all who gather around him. Everyone will recognize the authority of the Torah and will see it in Mashiach's life and so, everyone will fear him and will bring tribute to him, thus doing the will of Adonai, the only One God. And this is the revelation behind the "irrelevant" fact reported by Matthew.

The Word of God amazes me, there is nothing like it in this life. This prophecy reveals to us that Yeshua, besides being Mashiach Ben Yosef, is also Mashiach Ben David, that the royal authority of the house of David is upon his shoulders, that he will be raised up by God and that all peoples will gather around him. This prophecy also teaches us that he will teach how everyone should serve God, and this teaching will be based in the only existing truth, the Torah.

And that is precisely what those who saw him did not understand; and here we are, without seeing him, 2000 years later, by the mercy of the ONE WHO IS, understanding it!

Yeshua said to him, Thomas, because you have seen me, you have believed: blessed are they that have not seen, and yet have believed.
John 20:29

ELI ELI

אֵלִי אֵלִי לָמָה עֲזַבְתָּנִי רָחוֹק מִישׁוּעָתִי דִּבְרֵי שַׁאֲגָתִי

ELI ELI, why have You forsake me; why so far from delivering me and from my anguished roaring?

Psalms 22:2

Yeshua shouted aloud, in the holy language (Hebrew): ELI ELI, why did you forsake me?

Matthew 27:46

Christian theology teaches that their jesus, before his death, pronounced ELI ELI LAMAH SABACHTANI in Aramaic. However, the original gospel of Matthew, which was written in Hebrew, is categorical when it states that Yeshua pronounced such words in Hebrew; in the holy language, he said: ELI ELI LAMAH AZAVTANI, using exactly the same words found in Psalm 22:2 .

ELI ELI, why did you forsake me? - This is an outcry that represents the people of the Kingdom of Israel as a whole, for they continue in exile as one man. Eli, Eli, is repeated, for the first one represents the calling to God and the second one represents His work of redemption, meaning: You are my rock and my strength, why have you forsaken me?

Radak, Tehilim 22

According to Rabbi David Kimhi, known as Radak, this appeal to God found in the book of Psalms is a prophetic prayer to be said by the descendants of the lost people of Israel, the very ones Yeshua came after, people that will find out who they are when Mashiach Ben David is at the door. He also claims that this people is like one man, that is, all descendants of these tribes are as one, for they have something in common, the divine spark that was given to their ascendants at the foot of Mount Sinai as our sages teach.

Yeshua, by uttering these words, not only says a prayer, not only teaches us that we should seek God even in the most distressed moments that we go through, but he reveals to us, through rabbinic understanding, that he says a prayer for the lost tribes of God, Israel; Yeshua, before his death, intercedes for those who were the targets of his death, just as the prophet himself confirms:

וְהוּא חֵטְא־רַבִּים נָשָׂא וְלַפֹּשְׁעִים יַפְגִּיעַ

...Whereas he bore the sin of many And made intercession for the rebels.

Isaiah 53:12b

Yeshua takes the blame for the idolatry of the people of Israel, intercedes for them and so, a chance for God's word to return to their hands is given to them. He puts himself in the place of those people who have forgotten the true God, His will, and His name. The "forsake me" does not refer to him, for certainly God would have never forsaken him, but rather it refers to the people, the tribes; in their place, Yeshua prays what these people should have been praying, this is his real intercession.

In addition, in a hidden way, this Yeshua's prayer can confirm something that Peter teaches to the Jews in one of his letters:

Who did no sin, neither was guile found in his mouth.

I Peter 2:22

The sum of the letters of Psalm 22:2 is equal to 2776, which is the same value as another verse written by King Solomon:

כִּי־אֱמֶת יֶהְגֶּה חִכִּי וְתוֹעֲבַת שְׂפָתַי רֶשַׁע

My mouth utters truth; Wickedness is abhorrent to my lips.
Proverbs 8:7

*EMET - TRUTH - the mouth that only truth comes out is
the mouth that teaches the truth behind the Torah.*
Metzudat David, Mishlei 8

Another thing that this prayer of Yeshua teaches us, according to the rabbinical understanding, which was Yeshua's understanding for being also a rabbi, is about his teachings of Torah, for what he revealed concerning God's Law is the truth about it and that was the reason for Peter's statement above. It is as if he cries out to his people: "Listen to me and learn and live what I taught".

*Take my yoke as your yoke and learn from my
Torah, for I am humble, I am good and pure in
heart and you will find rest in your souls.*
Matthew 11:29

*He went around all the cities and towers teaching
Torah in the synagogues and preaching the good tidings
and healing every illness and every sickness.*
Matthew 9:35

It is amazing how everything connects and how the simple appearance of Yeshua's words and works have revelations about himself and his mission that are never clear to common understanding. Finally, I would like to present a brief study about this "truth", about this EMET:

רֹאשׁ־דְּבָרְךָ אֱמֶת וּלְעוֹלָם כָּל־מִשְׁפַּט צִדְקֶךָ

Truth is the essence of Your Torah; Your just rules are eternal.
Psalm 119:160

The "word of truth" is the Torah.
Machzor Rosh Hashanah Ashkenaz 46

First of all, it is vital that it is clear that the "word of truth" refers precisely to the Torah. Both the psalmist and the Machzor that is read during the Rosh Hashanah celebration, make this very clear. Within the Jewish mentality, the term EMET DABAR (אמת דבר) - *word of truth* - is a direct reference to the Torah. But in order for us to go deeper, let's conceptualize what this "truth" would be, why it represents the Torah so well and why Yeshua is linked to it one the book of Peter.

TRUTH, in Hebrew, is EMET, one of the few words that has no plural form, for truth in the holy language, is only one. Therefore, the truth cannot be anything other than the Torah itself. But the best way to conceptualize something is to conceptualize its opposite, the truth is best understood when the lie is also.

SHEKER (שקר)

ש 3 + ק 1 + ר 2

= **6**

If we look at the Hebrew alphabet, we see that the three letters that compose the word SHEKER (שקר) - *lie* - are adjacent letters, they are one next to another. This shows that a lie is easily found, since it is always "near". Another thing in relation to this word that we should notice is its shape in Hebrew, the basis of the word SHEKER (שקר) is as if it were leaning on one foot, something unbalanced, something that could easily fall.

EMET (אמת)

א 1 + מ 4 + ת 4

= **9**

Just as truth and lie are two totally opposite things, so are their Gematria values, 6 for SHEKER - *lie* - and 9 for EMET - *truth*. Also in the Hebrew alphabet, the letters that make up the word EMET (אמת) are as far away as possible, being the first one, one right in the center and the the third is the last letter in the Hebrew alphabet, since truth is something rare to find and distant for many people, for how many people know and believe in the Torah? Unlike the word SHEKER (שקר), the basis of the word EMET (אמת) is straight, so it stands by itself, it has balance.

Emet and death

With an even more mystical analysis of the Hebrew word EMET we shall see what damage it can do if it is not well understood. As we have seen before, each letter of the Hebrew alphabet has an equivalent number. Due to these numerical values, certain letters are associated with things or beings, as in the case of the letter ALEF (א) for being the first letter of the alphabet and it is represented by the number 1, this letter is assigned to God Himself, for He is ONE. Alef (א) represents ADONAI (אדני).

Therefore, if we look at the word EMET (אמת) and remove God from this truth, by removing the letter ALEF (א) from the word EMET (אמת), we have only MET (מת) which means death. By this we understand that, although there is much truth in all beliefs around the world, the truth which does not have the God of Israel, who is ONE, even though they are true to some extent, they are truths that will bring only death.

Another revelation this word brings is its deep connection with the Torah. The first letter of the word TORAH (תורה) is the letter TAV (ת), which is the same letter as the word EMET (אמת) ends. If we have any "truth" other than the Torah, it would be as if we remove the letter TAV (ת) from the word EMET (אמת) and thus we would have EME (אמ).

This term means something like a "matrix", a nonexistent parallel reality, that is, who lives some "truth", whether it is any religion or concept formed by the minds of men, lives in a false reality, lives in a world of lies, a religion of lies, a life of lies, a concept of lies and such bring only agony, depression, disgust, disgrace and so on.

To end this analysis, it is interesting to look at how a Jew, a rabbi, a Pharisee, a sage, as Yeshua was, would understand this term:

> *Your righteousness is eternal; Your Torah is true.*
>
> Psalms 119:142

> *And His Torah is the EMET, for all His commandments are EMET and the reason for the existence of the world.*
>
> Radak, Psalm 119:142

> *You, O LORD, are near, and all Your commandments are true.*
>
> Psalms 119:151

> *The individual who is committed to the Torah may be called as Emet, for his reason for existence becomes a truth and not a false reality (EME).*
>
> Chomat Anakh, Psalm 119:151

> *And truth (EMET) refers only to the Torah, as it is written: buy the truth and do not sale it, as well as wisdom, guidance, and understanding.*
>
> Talmud of Babylon, Tractate Brakhot 5b

> *Reish Lakish said: The letter TAV (ת) is the last letter of the Saint's seal, Blessed Be He, and Rabbi Hanina said: The Saint's seal, Blessed be He, is the TRUTH (EMET - אמת), which ends with the letter TAV (ת). Rabbi Shmuel teaches that the Torah must be followed from ALEF (א) to TAV (ת) from the beginning to the end.*
>
> Talmud of Babylon, Tractate Brakhot 55a

The beginning of the truth

בְּרֵאשִׁית בָּרָא אֱלֹהִים אֵת הַשָּׁמַיִם וְאֵת הָאָרֶץ
In the beginning created Elohim the heavens and the earth.

Genesis 1:1

Although everyone understands that everything was once created, many still have a little difficulty in including certain abstract concepts within this "everything", such as kindness. Such a concept was "created" within our reality, because it is one of the attributes that represents the Creator, on the other hand, He also had to create evil, because without it, how would human beings understand His kindness?

The same is true about the truth. Before the creation of all things and when everything was filled by the presence of Adonai, the truth was not a concept but the only existing reality. When Adonai shrinks His presence, His light, in order to make "space" to create all things, He had to include in this reality the "truth" that was removed and the opposite of it. Since truth is the basis of everything and the most important concept, Adonai inserted it into human reality before all the other attributes that came through the "light", as reported at the end of the first verse.

In the first three words of the Torah it is where this action occurs, it is when Adonai brings the truth into our reality and defines it. This is shown to us in the last letters of each of the first three words from the very first verse of Genesis, as highlighted above:

ALEF (א) - MEM (מ / ם) - TAV (ת) = EMET (אמת)

This teaches us that the only truth is what is connected to Elohim, His Word and His will. Everything else, all the "truths" of men and religions, however true they may seem, are lies!

The words of Yeshua reveal to us a prayer for the lost sheep of Israel, he stands in the place of this people; We are also told that this prayer goes beyond a mere supplication, but it is a message; a message that his teaching of Torah and his sacrifice in order to bring back this people, are the truth of how the

Torah should be observed and lived, for it is the ONLY truth.

THE TOMB

וַיִּתֵּן אֶת־רְשָׁעִים קִבְרֹו וְאֶת־עָשִׁיר בְּמֹתָיו עַל לֹא־חָמָס עָשָׂה וְלֹא מִרְמָה בְּפִיו

*And his grave was set among the wicked, And with
the rich, in his death. Though he had done no evil-
doing And had spoken no falsehood.*

Isaiah 53:9

*Then two thieves were hung with him, one
on his right and one on his left.*

Matthew 27:38

*At evening time, a rich man named Yosef came, a talmid of
Yeshua. He came to Pilat and asked him for the body of Yeshua.
Pilat commanded that they should give it to him. Yosef took
it and wrapped it in a very fine silk garment. He placed him in
his own tomb which had been freshly hewn from stone.*

Matthew 27:57-60

Every single prophecy found in the Tanakh works with a different level of prophetic progression, that is, they reveal to us how God's will and His Torah develop according to human development over the centuries. However, there is something in all of the prophecies that does not change, all of them carry spiritual secrets hidden in their words that serve for all generations, secrets that teach those who find them the true will of God, the true plan of God, and especially, how He operates.

As with all the other prophecies seen so far in this book, Isaiah's prophetic words regarding Yeshua's death and burial could not be different. In a direct way, its fulfillment is clear, for the prophet says that Mashiach would be set among the wicked and Matthew tells us that Yeshua was hung between two thieves, then Isaiah reveals that Mashiach would be with the rich in his death and then Matthew states that Yeshua was buried in the grave of Yosef, a rich man; prophecies clearly fulfilled in the life of Yeshua, as taught by the gospels.

Isaiah also secretly tells us the real reason why Yeshua was hung in the midst of two thieves and why he was buried in a rich man's grave. But in order to see what is really happening in this verse, a thorough analysis is needed in the same way that some of the greatest rabbis tend to analyze a verse.

First I will separate the verse from Isaiah 53:9 into two parts, PART 1 and PART 2, then I will highlight the two most important terms in each part. In PART 1 there are two nouns that are the most relevant terms of this part, RICH and WICKED. In PART 2 other two essential terms, EVIL-DOING and FALSE-HOOD. Among all the words in this verse, these four are the ones that give the real meaning of it, and they are the ones that link the prophecy to the account from the book of Matthew.

In this way, we shall have the verse as follows:

PART 2		PART 1	
על לא **חמס** עשה ולא **מרמה** בפיו		ויתן את **רשעים** קברו ואת **עשיר** במתיו	
A2	B2	B1	A1

A1 - **רשעים** (reshayim) - wicked
A2 - **מרמה** (marmah) - deception

B1 - **עשיר** (ashir) - rich
B2 - **חמס** (chamas) - evil-doing

Now, with the help of Gematria, we shall see the value that each of these terms has and how they can be linked to other terms and passages found in the Tanakh. The first term, RE-SHAYIM, has the same value as a term widely used by the

Torah, something taken very seriously by God:

RESHAYIM (רשעים) - WICKED

ר200 + ש300 + ע70 + י10 + ם40

= **620**

TEHOROT (טהרות) - PURITY

ט9 + ה5 + ר200 + ו6 + ת400

= **620**

Purity, or purification, is a God's requirement throughout the Torah, and it is closely related to sexual immorality, temple work, ministerial work, food, among others. The reasons for purity and impurity are not explicitly explained by the Torah, only a requirement. But there are two very clear things about it, the first is about contact, when it occurs with something impure, it impurifies man, and when it occurs with something pure, it purifies man; the second is that God demands purity for those who want to serve Him. Those two informations are all that the Torah tells us about TEHOROT (purity).

With this in mind, two passages draw attention about this:

אִמְרוֹת יְהוָה **טְהֹרוֹת** אֲמָרוֹת כֶּסֶף צָרוּף בַּעֲלִיל לָאָרֶץ מְזֻקָּק שִׁבְעָתָיִם
*The words of the LORD are **pure (TEHOROT)** words, silver purged in an earthen crucible, refined sevenfold.*

Psalms 12:7

*Then came Yeshua from Galil to the Yordan, at the mikvah of Yohanan. And Yohanan was in doubt about submerging him and said: Is it more propitious that I be submerged by your hands and you are coming to me? Yeshua answered and said to him, permit it, because we are obliged to fulfill all that makes one a tzadik, them Yohanan **submersed (TEHOROT)** him.*

Matthew 3:13-15

Next is the word ASHIR (עשיר) - *rich* - and just like the first word, this word is also connected to another Torah word by its numerical value:

ASHIR (עשיר) - RICH
ע70 + ש300 + י10 + ר200
= **580**

KIL' LATEKHA (קללתך) - YOUR CURSE
ק100 + ל30 + ל30 + ת400 + ך20
= **580**

In the book of Genesis there is a very deep passage that uses the term KIL'LATEKHA and it is a passage that perfectly fits with the work of Mashiach:

וַתֹּאמֶר לוֹ אִמּוֹ עָלַי **קִלְלָתְךָ** בְּנִי אַךְ שְׁמַע בְּקֹלִי וְלֵךְ קַח־לִי
But his mother said to him, "Your curse (KIL'LATEKHA), my son, be upon me! Just do as I say and go fetch them for me".
Genesis 27:13

The next word is CHAMAS (חמס) - *evil doing* - and despite its negative connotation, mystically it has a connection with the idea of freedom; As absurd as this may sound, this is exactly what the Torah shows us:

CHAMAS (חמס) - EVIL-DOING
ח8 + מ40 + ס600
= **108**

OTZI (אוציא) - I WILL REMOVE
א1 + ו6 + צ90 + י10 + א1
= **108**

The verb "to remove" is often used by the Torah in reference to the freedom God has given to the Hebrew people from the hands of the Egyptians; among several verses where we see the word OTZI referring to freedom, we have the following:

וַיֹּאמֶר מֹשֶׁה אֶל־הָאֱלֹהִים מִי אָנֹכִי כִּי אֵלֵךְ אֶל־פַּרְעֹה
וְכִי **אוֹצִיא** אֶת־בְּנֵי יִשְׂרָאֵל מִמִּצְרָיִם

*But Moses said to God, "Who am I that I should go to Pharaoh
and **remove (OTZI)** the Israelites from Egypt?"*

Exodus 3:11

Finally, MARMAH (מרמה) - *falsehood* - which has the same value as a word rarely used in reference to the foreigner, that is, the Gentile:

MARMAH (מרמה) - FALSEHOOD
מ40 + ר200 + מ40 + ה5
= **285**

HANAKRI (הנכרי) - THE GENTILE / THE FOREIGNER
ה5 + נ50 + כ20 + ר200 + י10
= **285**

וְגַם אֶל־**הַנׇּכְרִי** אֲשֶׁר לֹא־מֵעַמְּךָ יִשְׂרָאֵל הוּא וּבָא מֵאֶרֶץ רְחוֹקָה לְמַעַן שְׁמֶךָ
*Or if **a foreigner (HANAKRI)** who is not of Your people Israel
comes from a distant land for the sake of your name.*

I Kings 8:41

According to the book of I Kings, this HANAKRI, this foreigner, is not a common foreigner, but it is someone who knows who the people of Israel are and approaches them for the sake of the name of Israel, for the sake of God's people, and they do that so they may be part of that people, that is, the foreigner defined as HANAKRI is the one who is grafted into Israel as Paul teaches in the book of Romans chapter 11.

Now, we just need to connect the terms; as shown above, A1 to A2 and B1 to B2, and thus we will get the hidden message from this prophecy and the reasons why Yeshua was hung between sinners and buried in a rich man's grave.

A:

TEHOROT HANAKRI (טהרות הנכרי) - PURIFY THE FOREIGNER

B:

OTZI KIL`LATEIKHA (אוציא קללתך) - I (GOD) WILL REMOVE YOUR CURSE

Striking, because such ideas have been widely quoted by new-testament authors. As we do not yet have all the answers, we must keep digging to find out who would be the ones who will have their curses removed and the reasons for purifying the foreigner.

Beginning with the curses, there was a person who understood this prophecy quite well, as well as its motives. Paul, based on this ideia, claims the following:

> *Mashiach has redeemed **us** from the curse of the*
> *law, being made a curse for **us**: for it is written,*
> *Cursed is every one that hangs on a tree.*
>
> Galatians 3:13

Unfortunately, Christian theologians has the habit of taking possession of what is not meant for them. Paul, a rabbi, a Jew and an Orthodox, whenever he speaks in the first person plural, in this case with the term US, he does not refer to the Gentile, nor to the Christian, not to the church, not to the Western world, nor to the Vatican, but to his own people, to the Jewish people and to the people of Israel.

By this we understand that the curse that Yeshua carried away was the curse that was upon the people of Israel, the curse by which they were delivered to the Assyrians and to the Romans and were scattered throughout the nations, and, as already discussed in this book, this curse came upon them due to the idolatry they practiced, both the one practiced in the desert as well as the one imposed by the kings of the Kingdom of Israel. The word law found in this verse is not the Torah, but rather the Jewish *halakhah*, which for Paul has become a kind of idolatry, for they are man made laws that replace God's real Laws. Thus we have one more proof that Yeshua came to the lost sheep of Israel, for by removing this curse which caused their assimilation, he gives them a new path to return to their real God.

The purification of the foreigner is confirmed to us elsewhere, this time by Peter, according to the account of Acts:

> *And he said to them, You know how that it is an unlawful*
> *thing for a man that is a Jew to keep company, or come*
> *to one of another nation; but God has showed me that*
> *I should not call any man common or unclean.*
>
> Acts 10:28

This shows us that God has cleansed the Gentiles, that is, God has opened the doors of the People of Israel to all those who wish to be part of His people, all those who wish to accept His Torah and His will. All who love His name and are His servants will be grafted into this people, but first, to be cleansed is necessary, as the Torah itself commands:

> *And the LORD said to Moses, "Go to the people and warn them*
> *to stay pure today and tomorrow. Let them wash their clothes.*
>
> Exodus 19:10

Before the people received the Torah and effectively became Israel, they underwent purification rituals, that is, the Hebrew people, as a foreign people at that moment, before receiving the Torah, which made them the people of Israel, had to be purified. The same thing happens again due to the death of Yeshua, the foreigner became purified so that he becomes fit to receive the Torah and because of that, to be part of the People of Israel.

Thus we see yet another mission of Mashiach Ben Yosef being accomplished, the removal of the unclean spirit, for his death removed the curse of idolatry that was upon the people of Israel and purified the Gentile so that he could accept the Torah and thus be grafted into the people of Israel.

We can see Mashiach Ben Yosef in this Isaiah's prophecy in another way. The terms used by the prophet are RESHAYIM (רשעים), ASHIR (עשיר), CHAMAS (חמס) and MARMAH (מרמה), respectively they have the numerical values 620 (6 + 2 = **8**), 580, 108 and 285. It's possible to see the number 8 on all of them somehow, a number that represents this facet of Mashiach:

MASHIACH BEN YOSEF (משיח בן יוסף)

8ף + 6ס + 6י + 1י + 5ן + 2ב + 8ח + 1י + 3ש + 40מ

= **8**

430 YEARS

Another mystery revealed to us in the death of Yeshua is its correlation with the expansion of the people of Israel by opening the doors to the Gentiles. The passage from the book of Isaiah also addresses this subject. The total value of all its letters is 4274 which is the same total value of the letters from the following verse:

וַיְהִי מִקֵּץ שְׁלֹשִׁים שָׁנָה וְאַרְבַּע מֵאוֹת שָׁנָה וַיְהִי בְּעֶצֶם הַיּוֹם
הַזֶּה יָצְאוּ כָּל־צִבְאוֹת יְהוָה מֵאֶרֶץ מִצְרָיִם

At the end of the four hundred and thirtieth year, to the very day,
all the ranks of the LORD departed from the land of Egypt.

Exodus 12:41

Certainly, at first glance, it makes no sense with Isaiah's prophecy, much less with Yeshua's death and burial. But this passage has a strange statement that, if analyzed, can reveal what the eyes do not see.

This is a very strange passage, because the Torah states that the people stayed in Egypt for 430 years and historically, this date does not match the time the Hebrews were there and not only historically, since biblically we also have an apparent inconsistency:

And He said to Abram, "Know well that your offspring
shall be strangers in a land not theirs, and they shall
be enslaved and oppressed four hundred years.
Genesis 15:13

The problem we have here is the incompatibility of both verses, for God tells Abraham that his offspring would be in foreign lands for four hundred years and in Exodus, the Torah states that the people dwell in foreign lands for four hundred and thirty years, leaving a thirty-year gap; Was God wrong when He spoke to Abraham or is there a mistake in the Torah? Let's see.

In order to clarify, we should look at verse 41 of Exodus 12, where the Torah reveals everything to us when it says "to the very day":

*At the end of the four hundred and thirtieth year, **to the very***
***day**, all the ranks of the LORD departed from the land of Egypt.*
Exodus 12:41

The answer lays is in the question: What day is that? The Torah tells us that after Yosef became an important man in Egypt, his father, Yaakov, descends with all his house to dwell in that land. With 130 years old, the patriarch moves to Egypt with his children, grandchildren and all those connected with him. Levi, one of Yaakov's sons, had a son named Korath.

Another 130 years have passed after the arrival of Korath and his descendants in Egypt, when a son is born in his tribe and was called Moses. Moses, when crossed the sea, was 80 years old, thus totaling 210 years that the Hebrew people lived in Egypt. This makes things even more confusing. Let's keep exploring the story further back.

When Yaakov was born, his father, Isaac, was 60 years old,

when Isaac was born, Abraham was 90 years old and between God's promise of Genesis 15 and Isaac's birth 30 years have passed.

Promessa --------> Isaac --------> Yaakov --------> Egito --------> Êxodo
　　　　30　　　　　　60　　　　　　130　　　　　　210

30 + 60 + 130 = 220 + 210 (in Egypt) = 430 anos

Now, God's promise that Abraham's offspring would be 400 years in foreign lands makes sense, for this count only began after Isaac's birth, for this is the moment that Abraham's offspring really begins. Issac never owned a land, just as his son Yaakov never owned one, just as the Hebrew people in Egypt did not own the Egyptian lands, so, they have always been foreigners.

Therefore, the "to the very day" refers to the day God made the promise to Abraham. The day Isaac was taken as a sacrifice. The day the Hebrew people crossed the Sea of Reeds. In other words, that DAY, is the day of Pessach. Interesting or not, that "to the very day" Yeshua was sacrificed.

Let's note one thing, the association between the sacrifice of Isaac and Yeshua; the first served to turn the descendants of Abraham, the Hebrew people, into the People of Israel, pretty muck like the sacrifice of Yeshua served to give the Gentile the opportunity to turn from a pagan into God's People. The second thing to note here is that Isaiah's prophecy is also revealing the date that Yeshua would be killed, on a Pessach. That is the true message behind the prophecy that he would be hung among the wicked and buried in a rich man's grave.

◆ ◆ ◆

DISTANCE, AFFLICTION AND DESTRUCTION

אֹהֲבַ֤י ׀ וְרֵעַ֗י מִנֶּ֣גֶד נִגְעִ֣י יַעֲמֹ֑דוּ וּ֝קְרוֹבַ֗י מֵרָחֹ֥ק עָמָֽדוּ׃

My friends and companions stand back from my affliction; my kinsmen stand far off.

Psalms 38:12

And all his acquaintance, and the women that followed him from Galilee, stood afar off, beholding these things.

Luke 23:49

Psalm 38, written by King David, is a song full of sorrows and supplications from the beginning to the end. David's sins and afflictions are the causes of the pains he reports in this song. This Psalm gives a feeling that David was suffering from some sort of illness and the pain it was causing him made him remember his sins and thus, helped him to humble himself before God, at the same time he felt abandoned by his friends and companions.

In the book of Luke, something similar is presented to us during the account of Yeshua's death. When he was being hung on the tree, until the moment of his death, his friends and companions also kept their distance, and such an attitude makes a very strong connection with what happened to King David, making his Psalm almost like a prophecy of what would come to occur with Yeshua.

Since coincidences do not exist, we should look at these experiences David reported as prophetic, however, this could also make things very strange, because for what reason this kind of prophecy was given, I mean, besides another confirmation from the Tanakh about the life of Yeshua, what is the relevance to report that the companions of Yeshua did keep their distance from him during his pain? Indeed, although it is a prophecy, at first it does not have a very spiritual relevance and wouldn't have made a difference if it was not reported.

Studying the book of Psalms is not easy, as it is the most mystical book in the entire bible. In its words there are deep spiritual secrets, and it is upon them that we should look for the reasons why the same situation that occurred with David also occurred with Yeshua.

The fact that Yeshua's companions had kept their distance was spiritually important, for at the time when he was in distress, something spiritual was taking place, something so deep and so high that no man could approach anyone who accomplishes such a relevant mission. In order to clarify it, let's look deeper into the words of King David.

With a word by word analysis, it is possible to make connections with other words that share the same numerical value, as well as different verb conjugations. Let's look one by one, as well as which word these terms are linked to by their values:

אֹהֲבַ֨י ׀ וְרֵעַ֗י מִנֶּ֣גֶד נִגְעִ֣י יַעֲמֹ֑דוּ וּ֝קְרוֹבַ֗י מֵרָחֹ֥ק עָמָֽדוּ

Psalms 38:12

The first word that appears is OHAVAI (אהבי), which means "my friends" or "my beloved":

OHAVAI (אהבי) - MY FRIENDS

א 1 + ה 5 + ב 2 + י 10

= **18**

There is a well known word that has this same numerical value:

CHET (חטא) - SIN
ח 8 + ט 9 + א 1
= **18**

From this we learn that sin is directly linked to friendships, that is, friends can lead man to sin, as well as take him away from the sin, it all depends on how that person chooses his friendships.

The second word is RE'AY (רעי), which can be translated as "my companions" or "my partners":

RE'AY (רעי) - MY COMPANIONS
ר 200 + ע 70 + י 10
= **280**

280 is the same numerical value of something that King David was going through when he composed this Psalm:

YISER (ייסר) - AGONY
ר 200 + ס 60 + י 10 + י 10
= **280**

Next comes the term MINGED (מנגד) which in a direct translation means something that is on the opposite side, something that keeps a distance:

MINGED (מנגד) - OPPOSITE
מ 40 + נ 50 + ג 3 + ד 4
= **97**

Interesting, because the only word I found with this value that made any sense here is a term that apparently has nothing to do with it:

EL'EINU (אלינו) - TO US
א 1 + ל 30 + י 10 + נ 50 + ו 6

= **97**

Next is NIG'YI (נגעי) which is a contraction of the words NEGA SHELI (נגע שלי) which means MY AFFLICTION:

NEGA SHELI (נגע שלי) - MY AFFLICTION
נ5 + ג3 + ע7 + ש3 + ל3 + י1
= **22**

The number 22 is also the value of the word NILKACHIM (נִלקחים). NILKACHIM is the conjugation of the third person plural in the present tense of the verb LEHILAKACH (להלקח) which means "to be taken".

NILKACHIM (נלקחים) - ARE TAKEN
נ5 + ל3 + ק1 + ח8 + י1 + ם4
= **22**

Moving on, the next word is YAM'DU (יעמדו) which is the future form of the verb LA'AMOD (לעמוד) that means "to stand still" or "to remain still" at a certain point:

YAM'DU (יעמדו) - THEY WILL STAND STILL
י1 + ע7 + מ4 + ד4 + ו6
= **4**

Due to the value of this word being 4, we understand that there is a negative meaning behind it, something that can be cabalistically linked with tragedy, death or destruction:

HERES (הרס) - DESTRUCTION/DEATH
ה5 + ר2 + ס6
= **4**

The sixth word is KROVAI (קרובי) which is "my neighbors", but the word for someone who is close, as used here - KAROV (קרוב) - has the root formed by the letters KUF (ק), RESH (ר) and BET (ב). These three letters also form the root of the word KORBAN (קורבן), which means SACRIFICE.

MERAHOK (מרחק), which means something that is far away, has the same value as the word MASHACH (משח):

MERAHOK (מרחק) - FAR AWAY

40מ + 200ר + 8ח + 100ק

= **348**

MASHACH (משח) - ANOINTED

40מ + 300ש + 8ח

= **348**

MASHACH (משח) means "anointed" and has the same root as the word MASHIACH (משיח).

Finally AMADU (עמדו) which is from the same verb seen above LA'AMOD (לעמוד), but by calculating the verb conjugation as presented in this verse, we have:

AMADU (עמדו) - THEY STOOD STILL

7ע + 4מ + 4ד + 6ı

= **3**

3 is exactly the value of one of God's well-known names:

EL SHADDAI (אל שדי)

1א + 3ל + 3ש + 4ד + 1ı

= **3**

With that, I would like to offer a rereading of verse 12 of Psalm chapter 38 through the substitutions of the words analyzed so far:

> *The sin and the agony that are (coming) to us will*
> *be taken away by the destruction (death) of El*
> *Shaddai's anointed sacrifice (Mashiach).*
> **Psalm 38:12 - rereading**

Most fascinating is that this verse also tells us which sins are going to be taken away. God's Name El Shaddai is a name consisting of three Hebrew words:

EL (אל) - GOD
SHE (ש) - That (is)
DAI (די) - Enough

So we see that El Shaddai means the God that is enough. From this we learn that the sins that this verse deals with and which were taken by Mashiach are the sins that take the place of God, such as religions, money, professional success, greed, false gods, and so on. That is, the sin of idolatry, for idolatry is often not the worship of entities, but all that man has in his life that is more important than God, hence the name THE GOD THAT IS ENOUGH, for if we have Him, we do not need to worry about what we will eat tomorrow, nor about money, nor about career, nor about having other gods, for He alone is what we need and nothing more.

> *And almost all things are by the law purged with blood;*
> *and without shedding of blood is no remission.*

> Hebrews 9:22

Although everything seen so far is very deep, this study still leaves two questions, from whom the sins were taken, from everyone? And why precisely the sin of idolatry, what does a life far from this evil do to man?

To answer both questions, I will use the total numerical value of Psalm 38:12. By a simple calculation we shall have the value of 1456. That same number appears within a verse found in the book of Leviticus, in only part of it, but it is one part where God makes a very strong statement:

אַךְ אֶל־הַפָּרֹכֶת לֹא יָבֹא וְאֶל־הַמִּזְבֵּחַ לֹא יִגַּשׁ כִּי־מוּם בּוֹ וְלֹא
יְחַלֵּל אֶת־מִקְדָּשַׁי כִּי אֲנִי יְהוָה מְקַדְּשָׁם

But he shall not enter behind the curtain or come near the
altar, for he has a defect. He shall not profane these places
sanctified to Me, for I, Adonai, sanctify them.

> Leviticus 21:23

The Hebrew phrase highlighted above has the same value as the verse studied, the value of 1456, and it is this statement that answers all the questions. The first is who's sin of idolatry were taken, well, according to the verse, are those who have ALREADY been sanctified by Adonai, for He claims "SANCTIFIED" in the past form. So let's look at another verse:

> *For you are a people **sanctified** by Adonai your Elohim:*
> *of all the peoples on earth Adonai your Elohim*
> *chose you to be His treasured people.*
>
> Deuteronomy 7:6

That is, we returned to Israel, which, as already mentioned, fell into idolatry and was scattered among the nations. No one knows who their descendants are today, they can be anyone in the modern Gentile world. But there is something that makes their identification easier, something that will not be dealt with here. So we see that the death of Yeshua was not to take away all the sins of the world or the sins of everyone, but rather a specific sin of a specific group of people who are scattered around the world, as I said, it could be you, me, Your neighbor, we don't know.

This is confirmed in the words of Luke when he claims HIS PEOPLE, namely Israel:

> *To give knowledge of salvation to **His people***
> *by the remission of their sins.*
>
> Luke 1:77

This gives us the answer to the second question, How should we sanctify ourselves as Adonai commands? Simple, by placing Him above all else, thus freeing ourselves from all idolatry.

To sum up, the distance that Yeshua's acquaintances kept from him was a "prophetic attitude" of what would happen after his death. This distance was necessary, for he spiritually was removing the sin of idolatry that was upon his people through his blood, this is why no one could stand close to him. By his blood he showed to both Israel and the world a God that is enough, a God who supplies all His servants needs, wills and dreams; so, Yeshua not only removed the sin, but he also taught how to remain away from this sin, though the understanding of EL SHADDAI.

YESHUA, THE PROPHET

נָבִיא מִקִּרְבְּךָ מֵאַחֶיךָ כָּמֹנִי יָקִים לְךָ יְהוָה אֱלֹהֶיךָ אֵלָיו תִּשְׁמָעוּן

*The LORD your God will raise up for you a
prophet from among your people, from among your
brethren, like myself; him you shall heed.*

Deuteronomy 18:15

*Then those men, when they had seen the miracle
that Jesus did, said, This is of a truth that prophet
that should come into the world.*

John 6:14

The fulfillment of this prophecy is proven by John's own words. He reports that "those men" recognize Yeshua as the promised prophet, thus dispensing further evidences that link Moses' prophecy to Yeshua.

Yeshua, a Jew, preaching to Jews, is recognized as a prophet; though it seems a simple statement, it hides a lot of informations behind it. First of all, we must understand how the Jews define someone as a prophet and how these definitions led "those men" to this conclusion; knowing those topics will surely lead us to deep revelations about Yeshua's personal life. In order for a coherent interpretation to be possible, we need to pay attention to some commentaries from our sages.

Before I begin, I must point out three terms found in this seen-above passage of Deuteronomy; the first is K'MONI (כמוני) - *like myself* - the second is MIKIRBEIKHA (מקרבך) - *from among your people* - and the last is MEACHEIKHA (מאחך) - *from among your brethren*. On these three terms we will find three characteristics of Yeshua that led "those men" to recognize him as a prophet.

The meaning of the word K'MONI (כמוני) - like myself - is restrictive. Any prophet should only be recognized as a prophet when he does not add or remove anything from the Torah. If the prophet declares that any law of the Torah is permanently abrogated, the people should not follow his instructions, since our faith in the prophets is not based on the miracles they perform, but on their lifestyle. The reason we recognize Moses as a prophet is given by his communication with God, thus giving birth to the Torah.

Rabbeinu Bahya, Devarim 18

Moses declares K'MONI (כמוני) - like myself - for he teaches that prophets must show an equal faith in Adonai and in the Torah.

Rashbam, Deuteronomy 18:15

The Jewish faith, which is the basis and the essence for the recognition of all prophets in the bible, states that one can only be recognized as a prophet through his Torah lifestyle and not through the miracles he performs. Rabbi Ibn Ezra differentiates between the prophet who follows the Torah and the prophet who does not follow the Torah:

K'MONI (כמוני) - like myself - represents the prophet who follows the Torah, otherwise it is only a soothsayer.

Ibn Ezra, Deuteronomy 18:15

Those men who recognized Yeshua as a prophet certainly came to this conclusion after witnessing some of his miracles as John's states, but what led them to truly believe in it was the lifestyle Yeshua led, the lifestyle established by the Torah and the way he taught it.

Many wonder how to define a prophet of God from a false

prophet; well, this is the clearest way possible, for the prophet who comes from God will live a life in accordance to what the Creator established as law, he should also teach it, study it and live it out of love. Many still teach that jesus lived the law in order to this law to be consummated in himself, thus freeing his followers from the yoke of following it, However, the real Yeshua teaches something quite different:

> *At that time Yeshua said to his talmidim: do not think that I came to violate the Torah, but to observe it in its completeness. Truly, I say to you that even if the heavens and the earth (depart), a yud or a nekudah will not be abolished from the Torah or the prophets and everything will be fulfilled. And whoever fails to perform some Torah Mitzvot, however small it is and teaches it to others to do so, will be called HAVEL (futile) in the Kingdom of Heaven and whoever observes and teaches Mitzvot of the Torah, great will be called in the Kingdom of Heaven.*
> Matthew 5:17-19

This prophecy of Moses reveals the lifestyle that Mashiach should have to be recognized as such; if it were not in the conformity of the Torah, he could never have received such a title, also, he should not be recognized as a prophet neither and much less as someone sinless. This is the first mission of Mashiach Ben Yosef, to teach, to live and to propagate the Torah. Another commentary begins to reveal to us his second mission:

> *A prophet from among your people (נביא מקרבך) - the superfluous word MIKIRBEIKHA (מקרבך) - from among your people - is a hint that prophets will always rise up for the benefit of the house of Israel.*
> Tur HaAroch, Parashat Shoftim 18

This second definition of what defines someone as a real prophet is very interesting, for it defines one of the works of Yeshua as Mashiach, his pursuit for the lost sheep of the house of Israel, that is, of the Kingdom of Israel:

> *And Yeshua said to them, I was not sent except*
> *to the lost sheep of the house of Israel.*
>
> Matthew 15:24

> *MEACHEIKHA (מאחך) - from among your brethren -*
> *he will purify through the Holy Spirit of Adonai.*
>
> Tur HaAroch, Parashat Shoftim 18

And here we have Ben Yosef's third mission, to remove the unclean spirit from the world, something that Yeshua did, both by his miracles, teachings and the sending of the Holy Spirit. What do we learn from this? Moses did not prophesy an ordinary prophet, but in Moses' words Mashiach Ben Yosef was hidden. Moses actually prophesied the coming of Mashiach, and this is how "those men", reported by John, recognized him.

The three terms found in the prophecy reveal where this understanding from the sages came from and how they came to this conclusion. A conclusion which connects this "prophet" of Moses with Mashiach Ben Yosef and his missions.

K'MONI (כמוני) - LIKE MYSELF

1י + 5נ + 6ו + 4מ + 2כ

= **18**

MIKIRBEIKHA (מקרבך) - FROM AMONG YOUR PEOPLE

2ך + 2ב + 2ר + 1ק + 4מ

= **11**

MEACHEIKHA (מאחך) - FROM AMONG YOUR BRETHREN

2ך + 8ח + 1א + 4מ

= **15**

18 + 11 + 15 = 44

MASHIACH BEN YOSEF (משיח בן יוסף)

8ף + 6ס + 6ו + 1י + 5ן + 2ב + 1ו + 3ש + 4מ

= **44**

Moses spoke of Mashiach, Yeshua was recognized as such for his Torah lifestyle, his concern for Israel and his purifying work. He himself speaks very clearly about all that our sages commented:

*Again he said to them, beware of false prophets who come to you in wool clothing like sheep, but inside are tearing wolves. By their **deeds** you will know them. Does a man gather grapes from thorns or fig from briars? Every good tree makes good fruit and every bad tree makes bad fruit. The good tree cannot make bad fruit nor can the bad tree make good fruit. Every tree which does nor make good fruit is burned. Therefore it is according to fruits, that is, by their deeds, you will know them. Because not everyone who says unto me, lord, will enter the kingdom of heaven, but the one who does the will of my father who is in heaven will enter the kingdom of heaven. Many will say to me in that day, lord, lord, did we not prophesy in your name, and in your name we have cast out demons, and have not done many signs in your name? And then I will say to them: I never knew you, depart from, all who do not practice the Law (Torah).*

Matthew 7:15-23

Yeshua teaches that the prophet is recognized by his deeds, which in Hebrew is MA'ASSEH, such term, within rabbinic language, refers to the observance of the Torah, something which he himself confirms at the end of verse 23.

RECOGNIZING THE IDOLATRY

אַל־יִשְׂמְחוּ־לִי אֹיְבַי שֶׁקֶר שֹׂנְאַי חִנָּם יִקְרְצוּ־עָיִן

Let not my treacherous enemies rejoice over me, or those who hate me without a cause wink their eyes.

Psalms 35:19

If I had not done among them the works which none other man did, they had not had sin: but now have they both seen and hated both me and my Father. But this comes to pass, that the word might be fulfilled that is written in their law, They hated me without a cause.

John 15:24-25

If there is something very strong in Christianity that has always struck me is the hatred that many have for the Torah, or the Law, and the slander that many theologians and pastors do about it. Lack of understanding of the word and the strong human manipulation that exist in many churches increasingly push people away from the true God for a cheap self-help or selfish resolutions of personal problems.

According to the first chapter of the Gospel of John, in its original language, Hebrew, and not in the translations we have in the Western languages, he makes a Midrash between Yeshua and the Torah in its beginning, when he states that the word was made flesh. Within rabbinic language, John is saying that Yeshua lived the Torah so intimately and truly that it was as if he, Yeshua, were the living Torah, the very personification of how God's will should be observed. Through this understanding that John presents to us in the first chapter of his book, we can understand that the intimacy of Yeshua and the Torah is so deep that it is as if they were both as one.

Now back to the prophecy in Psalms, by Gematria it has a total numerical value of 2053, the same value that the verse 3 of chapter 25 of the book of Numbers has, which will explain to us why Yeshua was so hated, as well as why Torah is so hated:

וַיִּצָּמֶד יִשְׂרָאֵל לְבַעַל פְּעוֹר וַיִּחַר־אַף יְהוָה בְּיִשְׂרָאֵל
And Israel joined himself to baal peor: and the anger
of the LORD was kindled against Israel.

Numbers 25:3

Hate and anger, very similar feelings, but here reveals the reason for all these feelings, idolatry. baal peor, a false god, which the people of Israel began to worship was the cause of Adonai's anger, the same was true concerning the Kingdom of Israel when its dispersion took place, and so did it happen in the time of Yeshua, when many obeyed the human laws more than the Torah itself, exactly the same thing we can see now a days in various religions.

How to recognize idolatry? Easy, just look at how they hated Yeshua who was the living Torah, just as they hated God's true will because of human and religious laws. Today, many hate the Torah because they think no one can follow the Law, or that it is cursed, or that it is a yoke, all because they simply do not want to follow it, for a god who adapts to the person is much easier than a God who requires that the one who wants to follow Him to adapt to Him; such a false god generates much income and a false feeling of comfort. Idolaters!

If Yeshua were here these days, they would do what the jews

and the romans did to him when he came, they would have hated him.

He who denies the Torah admits idolatry.

Rashi, Deuteronomy 18

It is through the Torah that one is able to recognize the idolatry and the idolaters, no matter how "holy" they may seem.

THE KASHER SANCTUARY

שֹׁמֵר כָּל־עַצְמוֹתָיו אַחַת מֵהֵנָּה לֹא נִשְׁבָּרה

Keeping all his bones intact, not one of them being broken.
Psalms 34:21

Then came the soldiers, and broke the legs of the first, and of the other which was crucified with him. But when they came to Jesus, and saw that he was dead already, they broke not his legs.
John 19:32-33

KASHER

The kashrut, or the kosher diet, is the diet stipulated by the Torah as described in chapter 11 of the book of Leviticus. This diet deals primarily with protein inputs and some details that address fruits, grains and vegetables. On top of these divine Laws, the rabbis suggested numerous interpretations and on top of these interpretations, thousands of human rules and laws were created.

Many look at the dietary rules of the most orthodox Jews and think that such customs are found in the Torah, such as the fire that prepares food can only be lit by a Jew or the prohibition of mixing meat and milk. Such habits are but customs that became human laws and they are not direct determinations stipulated by God.

On the other hand, the Christian world believes and propagates the idea that such commandments have been abolished, or they are only for Jews. Such an idea could not be more erroneous, for when God gave His Torah, He did not give it to the Jews, but to the people of Israel; every man who desires to be grafted into this olive tree must inevitably understand and observe the diet stipulated by the Creator. However, kashrut is not the topic I will address here, but rather the word "kasher" and its meaning, so we can understand some details concerning the prophecy above.

Kasher, in a more straightforward translation, means something like "propitious", something that is not inappropriate, and although it is a term most commonly used for food, it serves to all that is convenient and not convenient for man to do. For example, God forbids a garment that has cotton and linen mixed in its making, if that garment does not have it, then that garment is kasher; or also for example an item that was once used in some idolatrous ritual, even though it is an ordinary item, it becomes non-kasher and should not be used by those who serve the living God. That is, a kasher item is something that conforms to what God allows, an item according to the Torah. If the item is a non-kasher item, such as forbidden meat for example, it is called TREIF, which is the opposite of kasher, something that cannot be owned or consumed according to God's commandments.

With this in mind, it is possible to draw a parallel between what happened with Yeshua, the prophecy about the unbreakable bones and a passage from the Torah that addresses exactly the same theme:

בְּבַיִת אֶחָד יֵאָכֵל לֹא־תוֹצִיא מִן־הַבַּיִת מִן־הַבָּשָׂר חוּצָה וְעֶצֶם לֹא תִשְׁבְּרוּ־בוֹ

It shall be eaten in one house: you shall not take any of the flesh outside the house; nor shall you break a bone of it.

Exodus 12:46

Through this verse it is possible to retrieve various relevant information regarding Yeshua. The first point to be aware of is what kind of sacrifice the verse refers to, with a full reading of the chapter we will see that it is about the first sacrifice of Pessach it talks about; interestingly, Yeshua died exactly during Pessach. From this we learn the first secret by which his bones were not broken, for in addition to reveal that Yeshua would be killed on Pessach, it proves what many new-testament writers claim, that he was the Passover lamb.

> *Mar, son of Ravina says: if the bone is broken, the animal becomes TREIF, thus not kasher for sacrifice.*
> Talmud of Babylon, Tractate Chullin 11a

According to the Talmud, for a Pessach sacrifice to be kasher, it must not have any broken bones, otherwise it becomes treif and unfit for the ritual. The second point that the Torah imposes for an animal to be kasher, both for sacrifice and for consumption, is that after its slaughter, its blood must drain, so a sticking is normally performed.

> *But one of the soldiers with a spear pierced his side, and immediately came there out blood and water.*
> John 19:34

When Yeshua has his chest pierced with a spear, he had already given his spirit to the Father, that is, he was already dead and it is precisely at this moment that the blood of the sacrifice has to drain. The blood, in this case, not only served to forgive sin, but also to "kasherize" the sacrifice, that is, to prove that it is in accordance with the will of God and the Torah.

In short, when Yeshua did not have his bones broken and his blood flowed shortly after his death, God was showing that he was kasher, he was a lamb who was in conformity with the Torah and God's will, making him valid for that. This is alleged by the New Testament writers with the term "perfect lamb, for there were no sins in him". Now everything is clear, for if sin is determined by the Torah and he did not have it, it means that he lived and died according to the Torah. It is the Torah itself that proves that Yeshua was the perfect lamb by stating that his bones were not broken and his blood flowed after his death.

Now I ask, the Law that determined the life of Yeshua, the Law that made him sinless, the Law that made him the perfect lamb, was really abolished in the life of his true followers?

Blessed are those who understand.

THE TEMPLE AND THE BONES

The Hebrew word for "bone" is ETZEM (עצם). This is a term of the same origin as the word ATZMUT (עצמות), which means "essence". Our sages teach that sin, when it is part of one's essence, when its practice is common in one's life, that sin is so ingrained in one's being that it becomes as deep as one's bones, thus forming part of one's own personality. When this occurs, it would be spiritually like as one's bones will the very evidence against him in the judgement's day. The same is true concerning holiness, when man faithfully follows God's will, the Torah, his connection with the Creator becomes as deep in his being as his bones, for they are the part the deepest part of his body, the innermost essence of this man. As the prophet states:

*And they do not lie with the fallen uncircumcised warriors, who went down to Sheol with their battle gear, who put their swords beneath their heads and **their iniquities upon their bones**, for the terror of the warriors was upon the land of the living.*
Ezekiel 32:27

With this we can make some connections with the fact that Yeshua did not have his bones broken, for it would be as if his essence were broken, and this shows us that his connection with God, his holiness, which was given by the faithfulness to the Torah, was so strong that no man could break it. The

Sefer Yetzirah (the book of creation) compares some parts of the human body with different divine manifestations on this earth, in the case of bones, according to Sefer Yetzirah, they represent the wisdom of God, which reveals to us that even if everything in Yeshua has been assaulted during his execution, his bones, the divine wisdom of interpreting the Torah that was upon him, is irrevocable, and this fact connects him even more with the facet of Mashiach Ben Yosef, for one of his missions was to bring the true understanding of the Torah.

On the other hand, the bones reveal not only Ben Yosef, but also Mashiach's second facet, the Mashiach Ben David. One of his missions is the rebuilding of the third Temple. The courtyard of this Temple, as determined by God, has a plant as follows:

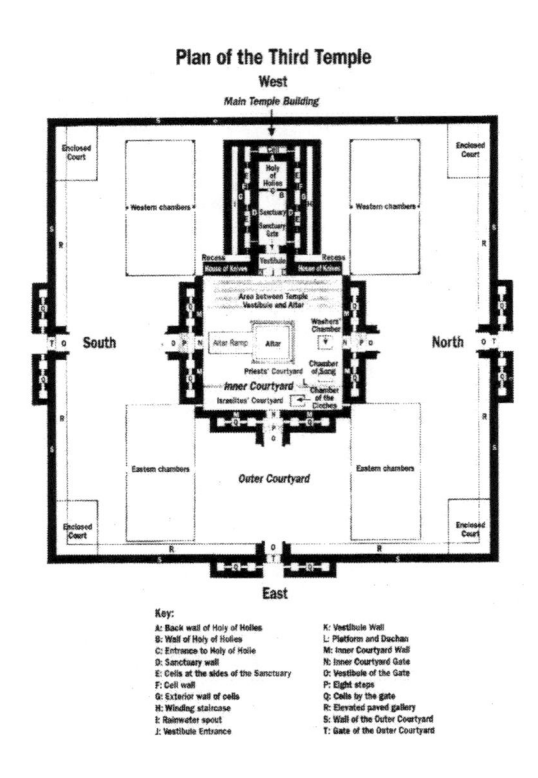

Plan of the Third Temple

The temple courtyard has a quadrangular shape with sides of 100 cubits each and the distance from the interior to the edge of the outer courtyard of 106 cubits, together they sum 206 cubits. The altar in the center of the courtyard has also a square shape, measuring 32 cubits by 32 cubits.

Bone is a solid substance that forms the central structure of the human body. There are 32 teeth, 32 vertebrae and 206 bone segments in our bodies. These numbers are the same as the Temple courtyard: 206 for the courtyard and 32x32 for the altar.

With this we can understand some messages. One of the reasons that his bones were not broken was because there is a connection between him and the Temple, which was conceived by God before the creation of all things; and this essence - ETZMUT (עצמות) - established by God between Mashiach and His Temple shall never be broken.

The second message is seen in the format of the word ETZEM (עצם) - *bone* - which ends with the letter MEM SOFIT (ם) and, just as the altar, also has a square shape. This teaches us that the account of the bones of Yeshua was mentioned by John as a message that the essence of Yeshua is the same essence as the Temple's altar has, for this reason his sacrifice did not necessarily have to be within the Temple, for upon his being was the spiritual altar itself, and this is why his sacrifice was the only one allowed by God outside the Temple since its building.

The third message we find here relates to why Yeshua had his left side pierced by a spear. Just as the word ETZEM (עצם) has a numerical value of 200, equal to the courtyard sides 100 + 100, the Hebrew word for heart, LEV (לב), has a numerical value of 32. This makes a direct revelation that the Temple will be rebuilt by Mashiach Ben David; It is understood here that besides Mashiach Ben Yosef, Yeshua is also Mashiach Ben

David, two different facets of the same Mashiach.

ETZEM (עצם) - BONE

40מ + 90צ + 70ע

= **200**

LEV (לב) - HEART

2ב + 30ל

= **32**

From what has been seen so far, some passages in the New Testament are easier to understand:

> *What? know you not that your body is the temple*
> *of the Holy Ghost which is in you, which you*
> *have of God, and you are not your own?*
>
> I Corinthians 6:19

According to Christian theology, this statement by Paul refers to "holiness" that the Christian must have, that is, one must not have bad habits that harm his body. On top of that, various rules of Christian Puritanism are taught as divine commandments, which have nothing to do with what the Torah defines as sin.

When Paul states that man must be the Temple of the Spirit, he is saying that just as Yeshua was worthy of being a sacrifice before God because of his obedience to the Torah and to the divine will, so must man, the follower of the true Mashiach, make himself worthy to become a living sacrifice before Adonai through the observance of His will; and it has nothing to do with the puritanism taught by the churches. This is the only way to transform one's body into a Temple to the Holy Ghost.

> *And I heard a great voice out of heaven saying, Behold, **the temple***
> ***of God is with men, and he will dwell with them**, and they shall be*
> *his people, and God himself shall be with them, and be their God.*
>
> Revelations 21:3

This passage from Revelations also becomes clearer now; when John wrote it, he made a comparison of the Temple with Mashiach Ben David himself; not only because of the Temple reconstruction, but what he really says is what has been talked about in this chapter, that Yeshua, as Mashiach Ben David, is the Temple itself. His royalty will bring the essence (ETZEM) of the one God among all men.

PERSONAL CHARACTERISTICS

Before concluding, I would also like to present two characteristics of Yeshua that are revealed through this Psalm of David. The total value of Psalm 34:21 is 2309, throughout the entire Tanakh there are two other verses that have exactly this same numerical value. And the most impressive is what they both deal with.

וַיִּקְשְׁרוּ עַבְדֵי-אָמוֹן עָלָיו וַיָּמִיתוּ אֶת-הַמֶּלֶךְ בְּבֵיתוֹ
...and they killed the king in his palace.

II Kings 21:23b

The first verse in 2 Kings speaks of a king who was killed instead of someone else. This leads us to two other passages in the book of Matthew:

*After, they set for him over his head a writing which said, ZEH YEHOSHUA NA´AZERET **MELEKH (KING)** ISRAEL.*

Matthew 27:37

When they were gathered together Pilat said to them, which of these do you wish that I should release, Bar Baesh or Yeshua who is called Mashiach?

Matthew 27:17

This exchange between Bar Baesh and Yeshua occurred because it is also part of the prophecy of the bones, for it is connected to the book of Kings, which reveals that the king had to die in someone else's place. The second verse with the same value is found in the book of Proverbs:

בְּפֶשַׁע אִישׁ רָע מוֹקֵשׁ וְצַדִּיק יָרוּן **וְשָׂמֵחַ**

An evil man's offenses are a trap for himself,
But the TZADIK sing out joyously.

Proverbs 29:6

TZADIK, a term poorly translated as "righteous", is an adjective often used by the Tanakh and the Hebrew language for the person who follows the Torah at heart, meaning, not by tradition but out of love, something very rare even in the midst of many orthodox Jews.

To understand who this TZADIK that was mentioned by Solomon is, we must look at the last word of the verse, SAMEACH (שמח) - *joy*. This is a word with a root formed with the letters (מ-ש-ח), which are the same letters that form the word MASHIACH (משיח).

By this we understand some things about Yeshua through the prophecy of the bones. The first is that he would die in Passover, that he would be a sacrifice in accordance to the Torah, that he was allowed to be a sacrifice outside the Temple for the altar was above him, that he is the king who would die in the place of others (Bar Baesh for example), that he would rebuild the Temple and that he is a TZADIK, for he lived the Torah and through it, he was fit as a kosher sacrifice.

Pretty simple!

◆ ◆ ◆

SEVERITY

כִּי־יֶלֶד יֻלַּד־לָנוּ בֵּן נִתַּן־לָנוּ וַתְּהִי הַמִּשְׂרָה עַל־שִׁכְמוֹ וַיִּקְרָא שְׁמוֹ **פֶּלֶא יוֹעֵץ** אֵל גִּבּוֹר אֲבִיעַד **שַׂר שָׁלוֹם**

For a child has been born to us, A son has been given us. And authority has settled on his shoulders. He has been named "The Mighty God is planning judgement and redemption; from The Eternal Father, the minister of peace".

Isaiah 9:5

This is one of the verses widely used by the church to prove Yeshua's divinity; we must notice that in a more literal translation, as above, in contrast to those that exist in Western languages, the adjectives that define this child change slightly. According to the original, this child is the minister of peace, who has a God-given authority and is the plan of the Most High. Very different from what is commonly taught.

According to our sages, this prophecy found in the book of Isaiah refers to King Hezekiah, because at the time that this prophecy was given, that king was still called as "child". All the attributes described in the prophecy, that he is God's plan of redemption and a minister of peace, make total sense when compared with the life of this king, as he ruled over a peaceful and prosperous kingdom, bringing redemption upon his people.

This all happened because, according to our sages, God strengthened him for this mission and it is this strengthening that this prophecy refers to, as the Talmud claims:

> *The eight names of Hezekiah are as it is written: "For a child has been born to us, A son has been given us. And authority has settled on his shoulders. He will be called Pele Yoetz; El Gibbor, Abiad Sar Shalom" (Is 9:5). The Gemarah asks, but why does we not see the name Ezekiah? The Gemarah explains: it was not given a name, but an appeal based on the fact that GOD STRENGTHENED HIM (hizko - strengthen - same root as the name Hezekiah).*
> Talmud of Babylon, Tractate Sanhedrin 94a

Despite the strong connection of this prophecy with King Hezekiah, some sages dare to say that this prophecy is in reference to Mashiach, an idea which is entirely plausible. As mentioned above, two adjectives are given to this child, the first is PELE YOETZ (פלא יועץ) - *plan of judgment and redemption* - and the second is SAR SHALOM (שר שלום) - *minister of peace* - the prophet also claims that the authority is settled on him and that he comes from the Eternal Father. On top of that, we will look at a teaching of our sages that associates this prophecy with Mashiach:

> *This verse does speak of Mashiach, for in Isaiah 9:5 all the attributes that demonstrate Mashiach's pre-eminence are revealed. PELE shows us his knowledge and wisdom of Torah and how through it he will judge for all good or evil all living beings. Being SAR SHALOM remote to his authority over all nations, it shows us the authority that is on his shoulders.*
> Iggerot HaRambam, Iggeret Teiman 13

As our sages teach, this prophecy speaks of Mashiach Ben David, about his reign, his authority and how his justice will be exercised. We must also keep in mind that the association with King Hezekiah is coherent, as this king is from the same lineage as Mashiach, the David's lineage.

However, there is still something here that calls my attention, the term used by the prophet PELE (פלא), which deals with judgment and redemption. This is because, on the other hand, we have a very famous term called CHESSED (חסד) - *grace* - which is very close to this PELE used in this prophecy.

Both terms, PELE and CHESSED, as well as they walk side by side, they both are also opposites. CHESSED, commonly known as grace, in a literal translation means both mercy and goodness; The CHESSED's mercy is given by God when man sins and the CHESSED's goodness is given to man when he obeys, but both are free gifts from God, for no man deserves His goodness or mercy. On the other hand, PELE represents God's redemption and judgment and unlike CHESSED, PELE requires merit, that is, it is applied according to what each man deserves. If man obeys God and follows His laws, he will receive redemption, if man is a person far from the will of God, then he will have His judgment. PELE works according to one's behavior. This teaches us what the reign of Mashiach will be like, it will be tough and firm, just as John relates in his book:

And he shall rule them with a rod of iron; as the vessels of a potter shall they be broken to shivers: even as I received of my Father.

Revelations 2:27

This "rod of iron" is precisely the right justice applied through the Laws of God that Mashiach Ben David will impose, his reign will be no bed of roses, it will not be for people who seek a god adaptable to one's will and desires, but it will be for those who are willing to annul themselves in order to adapt themselves to the true God's will, and all of this, out of love for the God of Israel; those will be together with Mashiach. But now I wonder, is there any way to find out if this prophecy connects Yeshua to Mashiach Ben David? Is it possible to prove that this referred "child" has a direct connection with Yeshua as many claim? Well, by the sum of all letters in this verse, we come to a value of 4434. Throughout Tanakh there are only 4 verses that also have this same numerical value. They are *Isaiah 45:9, II Chronicles 4:19, Jere-*

miah 36:27 and Isaiah 14:24.

As the subject treated in each of them does not make any direct reference to the topic addressed in this chapter, I will present these verses only in Hebrew, as follow:

הֹוִ֚י אֶת־יֹצְר֔וֹ חֶ֖רֶשׂ אֶת־חַרְשֵׂ֣י אֲדָמָ֑ה הֲיֹאמַ֙ר חֹ֜מֶר לְיֹצְרוֹ֙ מַֽה־תַּעֲשֶׂ֔ה וּפָעָלְךָ֖ אֵין־יָדַ֥יִם לֽוֹ

Isaiah 45:9

וַיַּעַשׂ שְׁלֹמֹ֗ה אֵ֚ת כָּל־הַכֵּלִ֔ים אֲשֶׁ֖ר בֵּ֣ית הָאֱלֹהִ֑ים וְאֵת֙ מִזְבַּ֣ח הַזָּהָ֔ב וְאֶת־הַשֻּׁלְחָנ֔וֹת וַעֲלֵיהֶ֖ם לֶ֥חֶם הַפָּנִֽים

II Chronicles 4:19

וַיְהִ֣י דְבַר־יְהֹוָ֗ה אֶל־יִרְמְיָ֑הוּ אַחֲרֵ֣י ׀ שְׂרֹ֣ף הַמֶּ֗לֶךְ אֶת־הַמְּגִלָּה֙ וְאֶת־הַדְּבָרִ֔ים אֲשֶׁ֣ר כָּתַ֣ב בָּר֔וּךְ מִפִּ֥י יִרְמְיָ֖הוּ לֵאמֹֽר

Jeremiah 36:27

נִשְׁבַּ֛ע יְהֹוָ֥ה צְבָא֖וֹת לֵאמֹ֑ר אִם־לֹ֗א כַּאֲשֶׁ֤ר דִּמִּ֙יתִי֙ כֵּ֣ן הָיָ֔תָה וְכַאֲשֶׁ֥ר יָעַ֖צְתִּי הִ֥יא תָקֽוּם

Isaiah 14:24

Remembering that Hebrew is read from right to left, note the last letter of each of the first words found on each verse, as highlighted above. If we put these letters together we shall have the word (ישוע) - YESHUA.

A wise association from our sages from this Isaiah passage with Mashiach Ben David, for it reveals to us his name, YESHUA. But we must notice that, unlike the church's claim trying to prove the trinity by the use of this verse, Isaiah is very clear by saying that God gave him the authority and he was God's will, thus showing that Mashiach is not a god, but rather God's plan of redemption.

◆ ◆ ◆

MASHIACH'S PRIESTLY STAFF

וְהָיָה הָאִישׁ אֲשֶׁר אֶבְחַר־בּוֹ **מַטֵּהוּ יִפְרָח** וַהֲשִׁכֹּתִי מֵעָלַי
אֶת־תְּלֻנּוֹת בְּנֵי יִשְׂרָאֵל אֲשֶׁר הֵם מַלִּינִם עֲלֵיכֶם

*The staff of the man whom I choose shall sprout, and I will rid
Myself of the incessant mutterings of the Israelites against you.*
Numbers 17:20

This is a passage that tells how Moses' brother, Aharon, was
chosen as the first high priest. Just as it is a story full of
mysteries, so the verse that tells it is full of mysteries. Despite being a verse that talks about Aharon, it also talks about
Mashiach, for it is a verse that deals with leadership.

There are several evidences that associate Mashiach with the
priesthood, such as the order of Melekh Zadik cited by the
book of Hebrews. But within these numerous associations
that exist, I would like to present a very simple, yet unknown one found on the verse above; if we look at the terms
MATEHU IPHRACH (מטהו יפרח) - *the staff shall sprout* - and do
its Gematria, we shall have the following:

MATEHU IPHRACH (מטהו יפרח)
40מ + 9ט + 5ה + 6ו + 10י + 80פ + 200ר + 8ח
= **358**

This is the same value of the word Mashiach:

MASHIACH (משיח)

$$\text{מ}40 + \text{ש}330 + \text{י}10 + \text{ח}8$$
$$= \textbf{358}$$

Therefore, we can understand that this staff that will sprout is Mashiach himself. But that still begs a question, as what Mashiach would this be, Ben David or Ben Yosef?

Let us look at the first letters of that term in Hebrew, as presented by the verse itself:

וְהָיָה הָאִישׁ אֲשֶׁר אֶבְחַר **בּוֹ מַטֵּהוּ יִפְרָח** וַהֲשִׁכֹּתִי מֵעָלַי
אֶת־תְּלֻנּוֹת בְּנֵי יִשְׂרָאֵל אֲשֶׁר הֵם מַלִּינִם עֲלֵיכֶם

Numbers 17:20

Separating the first letters of each term, we shall have the initials of which Mashiach this passage is dealing with:

מ - משיח (Mashiach)
ב - בן (Ben)
י - יוסף (Yosef)

We can draw two lessons from this single verse, the first is the relationship that Mashiach Ben Yosef has with the staff of Aharon, which represented the position of high priest. Together with the Order of Melekh Tzadik, this is another plausible proof of the authority that Yeshua had as high priest, even though he was associated with the tribe of Judah and not with the tribe of Levi. It is through his connection with Aharon's priestly authority, as mystically represented by this verse, that many of the New Testament authors called him as priest.

The second lesson is the representation of authority that the "staff" possesses and how it is connected not only with Mashiach Ben Yosef, but also, according to John, with Mashiach Ben David:

And he shall rule them with a rod of iron...

Revelations 2:27a

John speaks in the book of Revelations how the reign of Mashiach Ben David will be, he will rule the nations with an iron rod (which can also be seen as a staff), with hardness, applying the Laws of God all over the world. That is why, according to my understanding, both verses speak of the SAME STAFF (ROD), for Aharon staff proofs the priesthood above Yeshua as Ben Yosef and the authority of Yeshua as Ben David.

As he said also in another place, You are a priest
for ever after the order of Melekh Tzadik.

Hebrews 5:6

JOSEPH, JOSIAH AND YESHUA

JOSEPH

There are very strong connections between Yeshua, Yosef son of Yaakov and the Mashiach connected to his tribe, Mashiach Ben Yosef; as well as several prophecies regarding this facet. In this study I intend to bring to light, through what our sages teach, all these connections.

> *The tribes became involved in the sale of Yosef, Yosef was immersed in feelings of sadness due to his separation from his father, Reuven was immersed in feelings of sadness due to his sin, Yaakov was immersed in feelings of sadness due to Yosef. Yehudah was busy taking a wife for himself and the Holy One, Blessed Be He, was busy creating the light of Mashiach.*
>
> Bereshit Rabbah 85:2

This Midrash teaches that nothing is by chance, all the events that occurred in Yosef's life were under the total control and will of God, for such events made the light of Mashiach possible. Mashiach Ben Yosef is very well represented in the life of Yosef Ben Yaakov, so it is possible to draw a parallel in the history of both and see that the very history of Yosef's life was actually a living prophecy, it was that light of Mashiach that God was designing:

MASHIACH BEN YOSEF	YOSEF BEN YAAKOV
God's beloved firstborn	Rachel's beloved firstborn
Mashiach Ben Yosef serves his brothers before his death	Yosef serves his brothers until his supposed death
God saw the continuation of Israel's people through Mashiach	Yaakov saw the continuation of Israel's people through Yosef
Mashiach Ben Yosef was brought to his brothers by the angel Gabriel	Yosef was brought to his brothers by the angel Gabriel (the man at the field)
Hated by his brothers - Jo 15:25	Hated by his brothers - Gn 37:2
Criticized his brothers - Mt 3:17	Criticized his brothers - Gn 37:2
His father loved him more than his brothers - Mt 3:17	His father loved him more than his brothers - Gn 37:3
Was a pastor - Jo 10:11	Was a pastor - Gn 37:2

Was sent by his father to look after his brothers - Mt 15:24	Was sent by his father to look after his brothers - Gn 37:14
His brother plotted to kill him - Mt 12:14	His brothers plotted to kill him - Gn 37:20
His brothers buried him in a grave	His brothers threw him in a grave
Didn't say a word while being tried	Didn't say a word while being sold
His brothers had a meal (Pessach) while he was in the grave - Jo 13:1	His brothers had a meal while he was in the grave - Gn 37:25
Died doing God's will - Mt 26:42	"Died" doing God's will - Gn 37:23-24
Was sold by a brother - Mt 26:16	Was sold by his brothers - Gn 37:28
Some jews tried to save Mashiach's life	Yehudah tried to save Yosef's life

His garments were full of blood - Mk 15:17	His tunic was full of blood - Gn 37:31
His empty grave caused concern - Mt 28:8	The empty well made Reuven worried - Gn 37:29
Came out of the grave alive	Came out of the grave alive
Went down to Egypt in his youth	Went down to Egypt in his youth
Didn't receive his kingdom immediately	Didn't receive his kingdom immediately
His disciples came looking for him	His brothers came looking for him
His disciples didn't recognize him	His brothers didn't recognize him
Started his ministry at the age of 30 - Lk 3:23	Started his ministry at the age of 30 - Gn 41:46
Ate with his disciples - Mk 16:14	Ate with his brothers - Gn 43:25

Wasn't recognizer after he left the grave	Wasn't recognizer after he left the grave
Reigns in God's right side	Reigned in Pharaoh's right side
Was a servant before being made the king	Was a servant before being made a king
Provided nourishment to his brothers	Provided nourishment to his brothers
Was removed from the grave by The Supreme Leader	Was removed from the grave by the supreme leader
Will be the King of the Jews	Was the first king above the jews

This idea of Yosef's life being a prelude to Mashiach Ben Yosef is well known among Jewish scholars. We must observe the strong parallel that exists between what happened with Yosef and what happened with Yeshua, because it proves that he is Mashiach Ben Yosef.

Matthew's book contains a very misinterpreted prophecy that will now make perfect sense and will confirm everything that has been presented here.

> *Fulfilling what was said by Isaiah, the prophet, a voice calls from the desert to return to the ways of Hashem and straighten the way of our Elohim.*
>
> Matthew 3:3

קוֹל קוֹרֵא בַּמִּדְבָּר פַּנּוּ דֶּרֶךְ יְהֹוָה **יַשְּׁרוּ בָּעֲרָבָה מְסִלָּה** לֵאלֹהֵינוּ

A voice rings out: "Clear in the desert A road for the LORD! **Level in the plains A highway** *for our God!*

Isaiah 40:3

If we take the original version of the prophecy quoted by Matthew and analyze the words *"Level in the plains A highway"*, we shall have something very interesting. To do so, we must use the first letters of each of the three words, from left to right, as highlighted above:

מ - משיח
ב - בן
י - יוסף

(מ)MASHIACH (ב)BEN (י)YOSEF

Despite this prophecy, as presented by Matthew, seems to refer to Yohanan, in fact, it deals with Mashiach Ben Yosef, as it is he who will prepare a path for Adonai and not Yohanan, the immerser, as many believe.

Unlike the western versions, where the word "desert" appears twice, in the original, the second word translated as desert, is "plains". In the geological map of Israel, basically, we will see that in the south region is where the Negev desert is located, in the territory of Yehudah and much of the plains were where the Kingdom of Israel was, in the northern region of Israel. If we reread the verse of Isaiah again, it will be easier to know what the author of the book of Matthew was talking about:

> *A voice from Yehudah will pave the way for (towards)*
> *Adonai, (Mashiach Ben Yosef) will level a highway for the*
> *north (for the lost tribes) for (towards) our Elohim.*
> **Isaiah 40:3 - rereading**

> *Building a path and paving a way for the redemption of the*
> *exiles tribes is part of Mashiach Ben Yosef's mission.*
> Gaon of Vilna

When Matthew quotes this prophecy, he was actually declaring that Yeshua was Mashiach Ben Yosef and that he was coming to save the lost people of Israel from among the nations. Thus it is more than clear that Yeshua Ben Yosef is Mashiach Ben Yosef, the one who should come, teach and die in order for the Torah to reach the nations.

> *By Your arm You redeemed Your people, the children*
> *of Jacob and Joseph. Selah.*
>
> Psalms 77:16

JOSIAH

On the other hand, we have a king named Josiah who reigned all over Judah, he is considered the most righteous king after Solomon and the last good king who sat on the throne. Josiah is the protagonist of numerous achievements, such as the reform of the Temple, the deuteronomic reform and the revival of the Law in the territory of Judah. Many believe that it was Josiah who compiled the Tanakh as it stands today.

Just as the life of Yosef Ben Yaakov was a living prophecy related to Mashiach Ben Yosef, the life of King Josiah is also a prophecy, but in this case, related to Mashiach Ben David.

MASHIACH BEN DAVID	KING JOSIAH
Will rebuild the Temple	Rebuilt the Temple
Will establish the Torah	Reestablished the Torah
David's lineage	David's lineage
"a son has been given" - Is 9:6	"a son has been given" - I Kg 13:2
The righteous king	One of the most righteous kings
Will eliminat all idolatry	Eliminated all idolatry
Will fight in Megido	Died fighting in Megido
Will teach the Torah to everyone	Read the Torah out loud in public

The King Josiah is a "mirror", a reflection, of the work that will be done by Mashiach Ben David, for this reason there are several works that make associations between them. There is an interesting one that deals with their names.

> Six people were called by their own names before they were created, they are: Isaac, Ishmael, Moses, Solomon, Josiah and King Mashiach. Why is his name Josiah? Because he was a perfect offering at the altar and because he reinstated His Law. And how do we know Mashiach's? Well, we know that it is Yinnon, because he will raise those who sleep from the dust of the earth, for this one who is called Yinnon is as it was said: "Before the sun, his name is Yinnon".
>
> Pirkei DeRabbi Eliezer 32

These somewhat confused words by Rabbi Eliezer claim that

both Mashiach and King Josiah were called by their own names before they were even created. Josiah has this name, because his sacrifice was considered perfect and for the restoration of the Law of God, two things that are also part of the mission of Mashiach. Rabbi Eliezer still claims, as already seen, that Mashiach's name is Yinnon.

So that we can confirm all these associations, I will do the Gematria of the three names:

YOSHIAHU (יאשיהו) - JOSIAH
6ו + 5ה + 1 י + 3ש + 1א + 1י
= **17**

YINNON (ינון)
5ן + 6ו + 5נ + 1י
= **17**

YESHUA (ישוע)
7ע + 6ו + 3ש + 1י
= **17**

This proves that, in addition to Yeshua being Mashiach Ben Yosef, as seen in Yosef Ben Yaakov's life, he is also Mashiach Ben David, as seen in the life of King Josiah Ben David's life. The number 17 represents restoration and this is something that occurred during the reign of King Josiah and will occur a lot during the reign of Mashiach.

You are the God who works wonders; You have manifested Your strength among the peoples.
Psalms 77:15

שלום עליכם

Made in United States
Troutdale, OR
09/22/2023

13115953R00137